JOSEPH PRIESTLEY
Scientist, Theologian, and Metaphysician

JOSEPH PRIESTLEY
Scientist, Theologian, and Metaphysician

A Symposium Celebrating the Two
Hundredth Anniversary of the Discovery
of Oxygen by Joseph Priestley in 1774

Erwin N. Hiebert, *Harvard University*
Aaron J. Ihde, *University of Wisconsin*
Robert E. Schofield, *Iowa State University*

Edited by Lester Kieft *and* Bennett R. Willeford, Jr.,
Bucknell University

Lewisburg
BUCKNELL UNIVERSITY PRESS
London: Associated University Presses

Associated University Presses, Inc.
Cranbury, New Jersey 08512

Associated University Presses
Magdalen House
136-148 Tooley Street
London SE1 2TT, England

Library of Congress Cataloging in Publication Data

Joseph Priestley Symposium, Wilkes-Barre, Pa., 1974.
  Joseph Priestley, scientist, theologian, and metaphysician.

  Symposium held during the ninth Middle Atlantic regional meeting of the American Chemical Society in Wilkes-Barre, Pa., Apr. 23-26, 1974.
  Includes bibliographical references.
  1. Priestley, Joseph, 1733-1804—Congresses. 2. Chemistry—History—Congresses. 3. Chemists—Biography. I. Hiebert, Erwin N., 1919-   II. Ihde, Aaron John, 1909-   III. Schofield, Robert E., 1923- IV. Kieft, Lester, 1912-   V. Willeford, Bennett R., 1921- VI. American Chemical Society. VII. Title.

QD22.P8J67   540'.92'4   77-92577
ISBN 0-8387-2202-4

PRINTED IN THE UNITED STATES OF AMERICA

Contents

Preface

The Ninth Middle Atlantic Regional Meeting of the American Chemical Society was held in Wilkes-Barre, Pennsylvania, on 23-26 April, 1974. One of the special events during the meeting was the Joseph Priestley Symposium commemorating the bicentennial of the discovery of oxygen by Priestley. Three recognized authorities on the life of Priestley—Erwin N. Hiebert of Harvard University, Aaron J. Ihde of the University of Wisconsin, and Robert E. Schofield of Case Western Reserve University—were invited to present papers at the symposium. These three papers constitute a significant contribution to scholarship in the history of science. An important part of this meeting was a pilgrimage to Priestley's home in Northumberland, Pennsylvania.

What is there about the life of Joseph Priestley and the last home of this simple unassuming clergyman, teacher, philosopher, and chemist that makes them so important to American chemists and historians? Let us examine his life and what has happened since his death to find the answer.

Joseph Priestley was born on 24 March 1733, in Fieldhead, England. His mother died when he was seven years old, and he was raised by an aunt who wanted him to study for the ministry. He was ordained a minister, but, because of his liberal religious views, he was often in trouble with the congregations of his churches.

Even while he was professionally engaged in the ministry, Priestley became increasingly absorbed in the study of chemistry, becoming ultimately one of the greatest amateur chemists of his day. Endowed with an unusual gift for experimenting and observing, he prepared and investigated many gases. Observations at his residence near a brewery in Leeds led to experiments with the ''fixed air'' (carbon dioxide) that came to the surface of the fermenting tanks. He found that when this gas was dissolved in water, it made an exceedingly pleasant sparkling drink. This discovery of soda water led the Royal Society to present the Copley Medal to Priestley in 1773.

In 1773 Priestley gave up his ministerial duties and spent the next seven years as librarian and companion to William, Earl of Shelburne. This position gave him enough spare time to do chemical experiments and to write about scientific and philosophical-religious subjects. He obtained ''dephlogisticated air'' (oxygen) in 1774 by heating a sample of mercuric oxide (''red precipitate'') confined over mercury in a glass tube and using a lens to concentrate the sun's rays. The resulting dephlogisticated air was neither water soluble, nor was it flammable. When he tried to light it with a candle, the candle only flared more brightly. Nothing like this had been seen before, and Priestley concluded that this new gas was completely dephlogisticated. This discovery of oxygen was to be his most important contribution to science, but ironically Priestley never realized its magnitude or significance.

In 1780 Priestley resumed his ministerial duties as the co-minister of the New Meeting congregation in Birmingham. Here he took an active interest in current religious and political controversies. Priestley was never one to back away from the issues of his day and took strong positions on most of them. He paid for this zeal on 14 July 1791, when his home and laboratory were destroyed in the Birmingham riots. His books, writings, scientific equipment, and experimental results were all lost. Priestley and his family managed to escape, but fearful of personal harm they never returned to Birmingham.

After a few years, he realized that his situation in England would never again be satisfactory, and he decided to emigrate to the United States. His three sons, Joseph Priestley, Jr., William, and Harry, were already there, and Priestley and his wife decided to join them. They set sail from England on 8 April 1794; their arrival in New York on June 4 and their welcome by such dignitaries as the governor of the state and officers of the city was widely reported in the press.

Two weeks later Priestley traveled to Philadelphia, where, once again, his fame had preceded him. He was received by President George Washington and found himself so attracted by the scientific and cultural advantages of the city, including the Philosophical Society founded by Benjamin Franklin, that he was sorely tempted to settle there. Only the desire to be near his two sons, Joseph and Harry, who had established themselves in Northumberland, Pennsylvania, persuaded the Priestleys to leave Philadelphia and consider making their home in the country.

Joseph Priestley, Jr., had planned, along with several other English gentlemen, to establish a community in Pennsylvania that would serve as a rallying point for their compatriots, who were coming to America in great numbers. They thought that the emigrants would be happier in a society similar to the one they had been accustomed to rather than being dispersed throughout the entire United States. Some 300,000 acres of land near Northumberland, at the forks of the Susquehanna River, had been obtained for this settlement. Though this planned English community never materialized, Priestley's children decided to remain in Northumberland. In July 1794 Priestley and his wife joined them.[1] Today the trip from Philadelphia to Northumberland (160 miles) can be made easily in three and one-half hours. In Priestley's time the journey from Philadelphia to Northumberland took five days. They had expected the journey to be rough, but it was more difficult than they had anticipated. There were only a few bridges, and many of the streams were filled because of heavy rains. Several times they had to be ferried in a canoe across creeks. The inns were poor and generally infested with bugs. At Harrisburg, Priestley hired a "common wagon" in which he and his wife slept the last two nights of their journey. Dr. Priestley at first thought that Northumberland would be ''no place at all to live in'' and asked his friend, John Vaughan, to be on the lookout for a suitable house near Philadelphia. Priestley soon changed his mind, however, and was quite upset when Vaughan wrote that he had found a house. In his reply Priestley told Vaughan that his wife did not want to go back to Philadelphia; she had ''taken an unconquerable aversion to Philadelphia.''[2] He also wrote, ''. . .my wife and myself liking the place [Northumberland], I have determined to take up my residence here, though subject to many disadvantages. Philadelphia was excessively expensive, and this comparatively a cheap place; and my son's settling in the neighbourhood, will be less exposed to temptation, and more likely to form habits of sobriety and industry.''[3]

By the end of August 1794 Priestley had selected a site for his home overlooking the beautiful Susquehanna River. He wrote to his friend Belsham, ''I do not think there can be, in any part of the world, a more delightful situation than this, and the neighbourhood and the conveniences of the place are improving daily.''[4] Mrs. Priestley, too, was delighted with Northumberland and wrote, ''I am happy and thankful to meet with so sweet a situation and so peaceful a retreat as the place I now write from. Dr. Priestley also likes it and of his own choice intends to settle here, which is more than I hoped for at the time we came up. . . . This country is very delightful, the prospects of wood and water more beautiful than I have ever seen before, the people plain and decent in their manners.''[5]

House building was a slow business in those days. Among other troubles the Priestleys encountered was the lack of skilled carpenters. In April 1795 Priestley wrote to a friend in England, ''Nothing is yet done towards building my house. It is next to impossible to get workmen and the price of everything is advanced one-third since we have come hither.'' In May he wrote, ''I cannot make many experiments to much advantage till I get into the house I am about to build. At present I have both my library and apparatus in one room in my son's house.''[6] In September 1795, a year after he had selected and purchased a site, he wrote, ''We have had an uncommonly wet and unhealthy summer all over the continent. . . .On this account we have not been able to make bricks to build my house."[7] He changed his plans and decided to build a wood house. There was no seasoned wood readily available, so the freshly cut lumber had to be dried. Priestley described this as follows:

"To kiln-dry boards we dig a trench about two feet deep, the length of the boards and what breadth you please. We then support the boards with the edges downwards and so that when the fire is made under them, the smoke and heat may have access to every part of them. Two or three stages are place one over another and on the outside, boards to keep off the rain. In ten days they will be as much dried as by exposure to air in two years. We commonly kiln-dry ten thousand feet at a time. The firewood must be such as is not apt to flame, lest the boards should take fire, which sometimes happens. The expense cannot be much. A house constructed with such boards I prefer to one of brick and stone."[8]

Priestley was very impatient at the slow pace of construction. On 28 July 1796, almost two years after he arrived in Northumberland, he wrote, "My house will not be finished until next mid-summer: but I hope to get the laboratory finished soon."[8] In September with the project in which she had taken such interest still incomplete, Mrs. Priestley died. Her saddened husband wrote on 19 September 1796, "This day I bury my wife. She died on Saturday after an illness of a fortnight. . . .She had taken much thought in planning the new house and now that it is far advanced and promises to be everything she wished, she is removed to another."[8] In the following year the house and laboratory were finally finished. The laboratory consisted of a small one-story building attached to the house. It was well equipped and similar to his Birmingham laboratory.

Joseph Priestley, Jr., wrote in completing his father's memoirs:

Towards the end of 1797, and not before, his library and laboratory were finished. None but men devoted to literature can imagine the pleasure he derived from being able to renew his experiments with every possible convenience, and from having his books once more arranged. His house was situated in a garden, commanding a prospect equal, if not superior, to any on the river Susquehanna, so justly celebrated for the picturesque views its banks afford. It was a singularly fortunate circumstance that he found at Northumberland several excellent workmen in metals who could repair his instruments, make all the new articles he wanted in the course of his experimenting, as well as, he used to say, if not in some respects better than, he could have gotten them done in Birmingham.[9]

Thus conveniently situated at Northumberland, Priestley resumed the pattern of life he had led at Birmingham, experimenting for the greater part of the day. Having completed his *A general History of the Christian Church*, he finished his *Notes on all the Books of Scriptures* and many other writings. He published his *The Doctrine of Phlogiston established and that of the Composition of Water refuted* during 1800. The most important experimental work that emerged from Priestley's laboratory at Northumberland was the discovery of carbon monoxide, which he obtained by passing steam over heated charcoal.

A number of people, believing that Dr. Priestley's qualifications as an instructor of youth should not be lost to the country, decided to establish a college at Northumberland.[10] Priestley was appointed president and was asked to draw up a plan of the course of study he would recommend and rules for management of the institution. One building was constructed, which was later used for the Northumberland Academy, but the intended college never materialized. Priestley, in a letter to Thomas Jefferson, said "...but tho I proposed to give lectures *gratis*, and had the disposal of a valuable library at the decease of a learned friend (new, near so), and had it in my power to render them important service in various ways, yet, owing I suspect, in part at least, to religious and political prejudices, nothing more has been done, besides marking the site of a building these five years, so that I have told them I shall resign."[11]

Dr. Priestley died on 6 February 1804, so tranquilly that his son and daughter-in-law, who were at his bedside, were not aware of his passing.[12] The house was sold in 1815 to Judge Seth Chapman by Joseph Priestley, Jr., for $6,250.[13] For about a hundred years the house passed out of the hands of the Priestley family, it was bought and sold by a series of owners. Ultimately, the house deteriorated badly. Dr. George Gilbert Pond, professor of Chemistry and dean of the School of Natural Sciences at The Pennsylvania State College was interested in the history of chemistry, and thus in Priestley's house. Since Northumberland was only seventy miles from State College, Dr. Pond often visited the Priestley home and noted the disintegration of the old place. He was determined that it should be saved and restored, but there was no money available to do the job.

In 1919 the house was sublet and used as a boarding house for railroad laborers. There were rumors that the railroad wanted the area for a railroad yard thus necessitating the destruction of the house. Dr. Pond saw that some action must be taken at once. He contacted his former chemistry students, who contributed funds toward the purchase of the property.[14] Fearing that the house was going to be destroyed, Dr. Pond thought of moving it to State College. The trustees of the college indicated they would underwrite perpetual care of the house once it arrived on their campus, but no funds were available for moving it to State College. Luckily, the railroad project never materialized, and the idea of moving the house was dropped. Dr. Pond purchased both house and grounds for $6,000 in November 1919. He then planned to collect a restoration fund, but his death in May 1920 brought an end to the project.

Some time later the house and grounds were restored, and a one-story brick museum building was built with the funds collected by Dr. Pond. The museum now houses some of the instruments used by Priestley in his laboratory.

The title to the Priestley house was transferred to The Pennsylvania State College in 1932 under the terms of Dr. Pond's will. It remained a part of Penn State, removed some seventy miles from the main campus, for more than twenty years. But this arrangement proved unsatisfactory and efforts were made to have it taken over by the American Chemical Society or the Commonwealth of Pennsylvania.

The Joseph Priestley home was formally acquired by the Borough of Northumberland in December 1955. Representatives from The Pennsylvania State University, Northumberland Borough, and several Northumberland organizations participated in this important event. Dr. W. C. Fernelius, acting Dean of the College of Chemistry and Physics at Penn State and a director of the American Chemical Society, gave the keynote address. Mr. W. H. Wiegand, director of the physical plant at Penn State, made the formal presentation of the deed to Mr. R. L. Davis, mayor of Northumberland. Accepting the deed, Mr. Davis outlined the Borough's plans for maintaining the property. These included the formation of a general committee to represent the borough council and interested civic groups. From this committee an operating group was chosen to have direct charge of the Priestley House, and monthly reports were to be submitted to the council. Operating in this fashion, the Borough maintained the property and grounds for several years.

Then in 1959 the Honorable Adam T. Bower from Sunbury introduced a bill to the Pennsylvania legislature for state acquisition of the Priestley home and its maintenance by the Historical and Museum Commission. The legislation was enacted, and the home is now under the jurisdiction of the Commonwealth. A custodian is always present, and the home is kept open to visitors.

In January 1965 the Priestley home was designated a registered national historical landmark by Stewart L. Udall, U.S. secretary of the interior. The Pennsylvania Historical and Museum Commission began an $80,000 restoration project on the Priestley house in 1968 in order to restore it, both inside and out, to the appearance it had when occupied by Dr. Priestley. A formal dedication by the Commission was held on 18 October 1970 with representatives from the Commission, the American

Chemical Society, and the U.S. Department of Interior speaking at the ceremony.

The American Chemical Society has had a long association with the Priestley home. In 1874, on the one hundredth anniversary of the discovery of oxygen, seventy-four American chemists met at Northumberland to celebrate the event.[15] Dr. Charles F. Chandler of Columbia College was chosen permanent chairman of the group and thirteen of the most distinguished chemists in the country became vice presidents. At the final session Professor Persifor Frazer of the University of Pennsylvania proposed "the formation of a chemical society which should date its origin from this centennial celebration." Such an organization was opposed by several prominent men on the premise that there were not enough chemists, and probably never would be, in the United States to support such a society. In January 1876 Dr. Chandler called for an April meeting at New York University. Many of the men present at Northumberland in 1874 later attended the New York meeting, where they decided to form the American Chemical Society. The meeting at Northumberland in 1874 had planted the seeds that grew into the American Chemical Society.

In 1926 the fiftieth-anniversary meeting of the American Chemical Society held in Philadelphia included a visit to the Priestley House to dedicate the Priestley Museum, a fireproof building on the grounds of the Priestley House. This was erected with funds raised by chemistry alumni of the Pennsylvania State College. Dr. James F. Norris, then president of the Society, and approximately two hundred chemists traveled by train from Philadelphia to Northumberland to honor the discoverer of oxygen.

It is indeed fitting that the Middle Atlantic Regional Meeting of 1974 included a pilgrimage to the Joseph Priestley House. At the conclusion of the Priestley Symposium in Wilkes-Barre, more than four hundred chemists traveled to Northumberland to attend the Priestley Medal Award Ceremonies at the Priestley House. Dr. Bernard J. Friedman, president of the American

Chemical Society, presented the award to Dr. Paul John Flory, professor of Chemistry at Stanford University, for his pioneering research on polymers. The award, the highest honor in American chemistry, recognizes distinguished service to chemistry; it is interesting to note that Dr. Flory won the Nobel Prize in Chemistry later that year. This occasion marked the first time that the Priestley Medal had been presented at the home of the man to whom it pays tribute.

We are very pleased to make available to a wider audience the papers presented on the occasion of the two hundredth anniversary tribute to Joseph Priestley, "patron saint" of modern chemistry.

Lester Kieft
Bennett R. Willeford, Jr.

Lewisburg, Pennsylvania

NOTES

1. J. Priestley, *Memoirs of Dr. Joseph Priestley* (Northumberland, 1806), p. 165.
2. Anne Holt, *A Life of Joseph Priestley* (London, 1931), p. 187.
3. Priestley, *Memoirs of Dr. Joseph Priestley*, p. 127.
4. Holt, *A Life of Joseph Priestley*, p. 188.
5. Ibid.
6. W.H. Walker, "History of the Priestley House and the Movement for its Preservation," *Journal of Chemical Education* 4(1927):150.
7. Ibid., p. 151.
8. Ibid.
9. Priestley, *Memoirs of Dr. Joseph Priestley*, p. 194.
10. Ibid., p. 169.
11. E.F. Smith, *Priestley in America* (Philadelphia, 1920), p. 115. The original letter is in the library of Congress.
12. Priestley, *Memoirs of Dr. Joseph Priestley,* p. 220.
13. Northumberland, Northumberland County Deed Books. These show the various owners of the Priestley House and the prices paid for the house.
14. Walker, "History of the Priestley House and the Movement for its Preservation," p. 154.
15. S.A. Goldschmidt, "The Birth of the American Chemical Society at the Priestley House in 1874." *Journal of Chemical Education* 4 (1927):145.

Acknowledgments

Grateful acknowledgment is made to Harvard University Press for permission to quote from *The Overthrow of the Phlogiston Theory: Chemical Revolution of 1775-1789* edited by James Bryant Conant and also for permission to use as illustrations Figures 9 and 11, Chapter 2. We also thank Pennsylvania State University Libraries, Pennsylvania Historical and the Museum Commission for permission to use their photographs.

JOSEPH PRIESTLEY
Scientist, Theologian, and Metaphysician

Photograph by Ralph E. Laird, Bucknell University, of a Sketch of Northumberland done in 1798 by Colbert Maulevrier. Reproduced by courtesy of the Pennsylvania Historical and Museum Commission. Original in the collection of the Countess Paul de Leusse.

Joseph Priestley. Photo by Pennsylvania Historical and Museum Commission, Harrisburg, Pennsylvania.

Collotype photograph of Joseph Priestley's tombstone in Northumberland Cemetery, taken in 1874. This stone is still in place
but the inscription is now almost totally illegible. It also was
apparently cut off and reset sometime between 1874 and 1921
when photographs show the final line of the inscription at
ground level.

To
the memory of the
Revd D. JOSEPH PRIESTLEY
who departed this life
on the 6th Feby 1804
Anno AEtatis LXXI

Return unto thy rest O my soul for the
Lord hath dealt bountifully with thee.
I will lay me down in peace and sleep till
I awake in the morning of the resurrection.

IN MEMORY OF
THE REV. DR. JOSEPH PRIESTLEY

BORN MAR. 13. 1733
AT FIELDHEAD. ENGLAND
DIED FEB. 6. 1804
AT NORTHUMBERLAND. PA.
— ANNO ERAT LXXI —

RETURN UNTO THY REST, O MY SOUL, FOR THE
LORD HATH DEALT BOUNTIFULLY WITH THEE.
I WILL LAY ME DOWN IN PEACE AND SLEEP TILL
I AWAKE IN THE MORNING OF THE RESURRECTION.

New Tombstone of Joseph Priestley, erected in 1971 by the Northumberland Cemetery Association. It stands directly in front of the older stone. Notice that the designer of the new memorial has misread the Latin inscription of the original. Photograph by Ralph E. Laird, Bucknell University.

Priestley House 1970. Photo by Pennsylvania Historical and Museum Commission, Harrisburg, Pennsylvania by Karl G. Rath, Harrisburg, Pennsylvania.

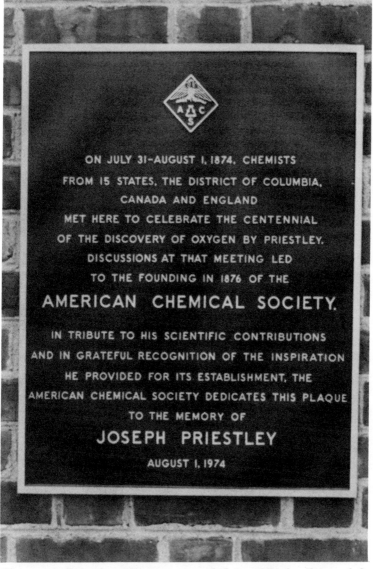

ON JULY 31–AUGUST 1, 1874, CHEMISTS
FROM 15 STATES, THE DISTRICT OF COLUMBIA,
CANADA AND ENGLAND
MET HERE TO CELEBRATE THE CENTENNIAL
OF THE DISCOVERY OF OXYGEN BY PRIESTLEY.
DISCUSSIONS AT THAT MEETING LED
TO THE FOUNDING IN 1876 OF THE

AMERICAN CHEMICAL SOCIETY.

IN TRIBUTE TO HIS SCIENTIFIC CONTRIBUTIONS
AND IN GRATEFUL RECOGNITION OF THE INSPIRATION
HE PROVIDED FOR ITS ESTABLISHMENT, THE
AMERICAN CHEMICAL SOCIETY DEDICATES THIS PLAQUE
TO THE MEMORY OF

JOSEPH PRIESTLEY

AUGUST 1, 1974

Plaque on Priestley Museum, unveiled in 1974 by Bernard S. Friedman, President, American Chemical Society.

The Integration of Revealed Religion and Scientific Materialism in the Thought of Joseph Priestley

ERWIN N. HIEBERT

Harvard University

Joseph Priestley was a natural philosopher with a remarkably broad range of intellectual interests and experimental skills. He held strong beliefs and adopted metaphysical positions that were vigorously defended at great length in his numerous writings. His life's objective, it seems, was to generate a polymorphic synthesis of natural science and revealed religion that would be, in form, intellectually acceptable and influential, and, in substance, rationally argued and true.

Neither Priestley's life style nor his scientific, philosophical, theological, or political thought are easily characterized. The kaleidoscopic Priestley was a man of many faces. He was a competent scientist—a skilled and imaginative experimentalist, but a cautious and conservative theorist. A major portion of his lifetime efforts was devoted to education, teaching, and writing. An unconventional thinker, often opposing tradition, Priestley was quick to grapple with the most controversial scientific and religious questions. He was a clever polemicist and pamphleteer, and a political liberal, but certainly no activist. Convinced that *truth* would win out everywhere, Priestley believed that candid and unbridled freedom of enquiry were to be fostered liberally and openly.

The main theme that I wish to stress in this paper is that Priestley was a dyed-in-the-wool historian, virtually incapable of tackling any subject without examining it in its historical context. In his emphasis on the primacy of fact as a source of knowledge Priestley was Baconian. As a Newtonian corpuscularian, his philosophical affinities fell on the side of utilitarian, mechanistic reductivism. His determinism was an imitation and extension of David Hartley's psychological associationism. He referred to himself as a ''confirmed necessarian.''

In the pulpit, as a dissenting preacher of the Christian Gospel, and in his theological treatises, Priestley was an impetuous rationalist. In his reference to ''rationalism'' Priestley meant not so much to place the emphasis on abstract reasoning, as on empirically and historically verifiable phenomena held together by sound (i.e., logically consistent) arguments. While still in his teens, he had progressed from Calvinism to Arminianism. That is, he had adopted the belief, contrary to the distinguishing feature of Calvinistic predestination, that salvation is open to free choice for all mankind. By stages he embraced Socinianism, or anti-Trinitarian views, that later developed into an expanded Unitarianism. However else one might wish to describe the various phases of Priestley's intellectual metamorphosis, he obviously, at the prime of his life, was a confident materialist whose enigmatic positive theology had become a source of puzzlement and irritation for churchmen and atheists alike.

Although Priestley's renown as a chemist was based mostly on his prolific experimental productivity throughout the decade of the 1770s, the greater part of his life was given over to the ministry and to writings on religion and its history. While it may be said that Priestley viewed his own explorations into experimental chemistry as something of an avocation, it is known that he achieved distinction among his contemporaries for his non-conformist views in both science and religion. The most conspicuous feature of Priestley's world view was that religion and science were compatible domains; that the scientific dis-covery of the works of God in nature were inherently in harmony with a historically sound interpretation of the word of God. Between the ''word of God'' and the ''works of God'' there was for Priestley just a natural partnership. While one may note that many distinguished seventeenth and eighteenth century scientists saw no intrinsic incompatibility between science and religion, Priestley may rightly be singled out from among them for having been so explicit about this and for having written so prolifically on the subject of the bearing of religion on science, or on natural philosophy, as it was then called.

Acknowledging that Priestley's scientific philosophy was so firmly rooted in his philosophy of religion, it seems appropriate to try to discover, more explicitly, in what sense he took revealed religion and natural science to be reciprocating branches of knowledge. To that end this paper is devoted mainly to an analysis and interpretation of the rationale according to which, and the context within which, Priestley integrated his conception of revealed religion with his fervent belief in scientific materialism and strict causality. It is appropriate, therefore, that we focus mainly on Priestley's religious career and writings in order to sketch the theological biography of a man who was theologian every bit as much as he was chemist. Accordingly, my objective is to furnish an expository account of Priestley's life as it pertains to his religion and to his religious writings, rather than to provide a new reinterpretation of Priestley's contributions. To put the various domains of Priestley's metaphysics into a meaningful synthesis, is, I must confess, a rather formidable undertaking— since he left a collection of theological and miscellaneous works that comprises twenty-six volumes, not counting his scientific publications.[1]

Born in 1733, the eldest son of a Yorkshire cloth-dresser,

Joseph Priestley acquired early in life a serious turn of mind and was exposed to Calvinist doctrines, mathematics, and a heavy dose of both classical and modern language instruction. After his mother died, Priestley, at the age of nine was adopted by a childless rich aunt. In his *Memoirs* he wrote concerning his "excellent aunt," Mrs. Keighly:

> She was truly Calvinistic in principle, but was far from confining salvation to those who thought as she did on religious subjects. Being left in good circumstances, her home was the resort of all the Dissenting ministers in the neighborhood, without distinction; and those who were the most obnoxious on account of their heresy, were almost as welcome to her, if she thought them honest and good men, (which she was not unwilling to do,) as any others. . . .
> Thus I was brought up with sentiments of piety, but without bigotry; and having, from my earliest years, given much attention to the subject of religion, I was as much confirmed as I well could be in the principles of Calvinism, all the books that came in my way having that tendency.[2]

Priestley once remarked:

> It has pleased God, in the course of his providence, to open my own eyes, after having been educated in all the gloom and darkness of *Calvinism,* and I am determined (in conjunction with my philosophical researches) to do all that I can to open the eyes of others. With this object in view, I am ready, with the apostle, to go through *evil report as well as good report;* and whatever of active life may remain to me, I am resolved to make the most of it; there being, as the saying is, *rest enough in the grave.* I have no higher wish with respect to this life, than to live, and die in the various pursuits in which I am now engaged; and I hope to rise to a scene of equal activity, and of equally pleasurable and useful pursuits, in a future life.[3]

The negative memories of Priestley's youth were punctuated with an exposure to a brand of dissent and heresy that led him to press his greatest efforts and stake his life on the "more rational notions of religion'' as he called them. Twenty-six years after he left his aunt's home, Priestley dedicated his *Disquisitions on Matter and Spirit* to one of the dissenters who frequently had been his aunt's guest: namely, a Mr. Graham—rational Christian, excellent classical scholar, and one of ''the most heritical ministers in the neighborhood.''[4]

Priestley's aunt and other relatives wanted him to attend a Calvinist academy. He refused. Instead, he entered the dissenting academy at Daventry with the aim of becoming a minister. At this time, we may note, that Oxford and Cambridge were closed to Dissenters. Priestley wrote in his *Memoirs:*

> In my time, the academy was in a state peculiarly favourable to the serious pursuit of truth, as the students were about equally divided upon every question of much importance, such as liberty and necessity, the sleep of the soul, and all the articles of theological orthodoxy and heresy; in consequence of which, all these topics were the subject of continual discussion. Our tutors also were of different opinions; Dr. Ashworth taking the orthodox side of every question, and Mr. Clark, the sub-tutor, that of heresy, though always with the greatest modesty.
>
> Both of our tutors being young, at least as tutors,. . . .they indulged us in the greatest freedoms, so that our lectures had often the air of friendly conversations on the subjects to which they related. We were permitted to ask whatever questions, and to make whatever remarks we pleased; and we did it with the greatest, but without any offensive, freedom. The general plan of our studies. . .was exceedingly favourable to free in-quiry, as we were referred to authors on both sides of every question, and were even required to give an account of them. . . .The public library contained all the books to which we were referred.[5]

During his three years at the Dissenter's Academy in Daventry, Priestley was most profoundly influenced by David Hartley's *Observations on Man* (1749). This psychological treatise, written by a Yorkshire physician and philosopher, aims to analyze and reduce psychic (mental) phenomena to physical explanations.

Hartley's theory freed Priestley from the rigor of piety. It served, he said, "to enlighten the mind, or improve the heart," so that it became reasonable "to embrace what is generally called the heterodox side of almost every question." As a result, Priestley was led at this time to adopt "the doctrine of Necessity."[6]

By the time Priestley left the Academy in 1755 he had accepted the heresy of Arianism. According to this doctrine Jesus had been created or begotten of the Father. He had not existed coeternal with God timelessly and without beginning. By 1755 Priestley also had moved to a more limited belief concerning the atonement. But, he remarked, "All the while I was at the academy, I never lost sight of the great object of my studies, which was the duties of a Christian minister."[7]

Priestley's first six years as a minister, at Needham Market in Suffolk (1755-58) and then at Nantwich in Cheshire (1758-61), were only moderately successful. He was unable to conceal his own views on some controversial theological matters. Besides, he labored under the difficulty of a speech defect. He managed to devote some attention to experimentation with "philosophical instruments," but mostly to keep up his diligent pursuits in theological studies.

> While I was in this retired situation, I had in consequence of much pains and thought, become persuaded of the falsity of the doctrine of atonement, of the inspiration of the authors of the books of Scripture as writers, and of all idea of supernatural influence, except for the purpose of miracles. But I was still an Arian, having never turned my attention to the Socinian doctrine, and contenting myself with seeing the absurdity of the Trinitarian system.[8]

As a tutor at the Dissenter's Academy in Warrington (1761-67), where he continued to preach as a dissenting minister, and where, in fact, he chose to be ordained, Priestley was singularly happy as a result of intellectually stimulating new contacts. His fellow tutors were all zealous Necessarians and Arians.[9] While teaching language, oratory, and civil history and policy, at the Academy, Priestley published several books on the principles of education and pedagogy. He met Benjamin Franklin who convinced him to write a history of electricity. He was elected a Fellow of the Royal Society.

Priestley's third pastorate was at Mill Hill Chapel in Leeds (1767-73). There he inhabited a house adjoined to a public brewery, and there it was that the excitement with experiments on fixed air [carbon dioxide that comes to the surface of the fermenting tanks] led him more deeply into experimental philosophy, in general, and into the subject of chemistry in particular. Concerning chemistry, he said he knew very little at the time. If true, we see from his publications that he acquired considerable expertise in various sciences in a very short time.[10]

It was also while he ministered to the "liberal, friendly, and harmonious congregation" at Leeds, that Priestley adopted, unambiguously, the position of Socinianism.[11] At Leeds he published essays and tracts on adverse criticisms to the reasoning of Saint Paul, on the doctrine of atonement, on family prayer, on church discipline, on the Lord's Supper, and a three-volume work on the *Institutes of Natural and Revealed Religion.*

For seven years, beginning in 1773, Priestley was the librarian for and literary companion to William Earl of Shelburne, and hence essentially at liberty to pursue his own experimental and intellectual passions. He discovered dephlogisticated air, published several volumes on *Experiments and Observations on Different Kinds of Air,* met Antoine Lavoisier and the Abbé Boscovich in Paris, and became a close friend to Benjamin Franklin.

While Priestley's erudition and writings put him in contact with the European and American scientific and philosophical world, his unorthodox religious interpretations were hardly looked upon with favor by divines within the heart of Christendom. It was notably inconvenient for most of his theological opponents, who might have wanted to attack him, that, unlike the French materialists and liberal Enlightenment philosophers, Priestley's ideas led not to infidelity but to a rational Christianity that sought divinity as well in nature as in scriptural revelation. That is, although Priestley's theology was unacceptable among the orthodox, it was not readily rejected on the grounds of its atheism or its espousal of antibiblical and heathen theology. While English critics felt that Priestley's theology was barely distinguishable from atheism, the French philosophers were puzzled to learn that an enlightened liberal, materialist, philosopher could believe in God at all.

The prevalent attitude toward Priestley's religion in France, and to some extent in England, is captured in comments relating to his visit in Paris in 1774:

I did not wonder, as I otherwise should have done, to find all the philosophical persons to whom I was introduced at Paris, unbelievers in Christianity, and even professed Atheists. As I chose on all occasions to appear as a Christian, I was told by some of them, that I was the only person they had ever met with, of whose understanding they had any opinion, who professed to believe Christianity. But on interrogating them on the subject, I soon found that they had given no proper attention to it, and did not really know what Christianity was. This was also the case with a great part of the company that I saw at Lord Shelburne's. But I hope that my always avowing myself to be a Christian, and holding myself ready on all occasions to defend the genuine principles of it, was not without its use. Having conversed so much with unbelievers, at home and abroad, I thought I should be able to combat their prejudices with some advantage, and with this view I wrote, while I was with Lord Shelburne, the first part of my ''Letters to a Philosophical Unbeliever'', in proof of the doctrines of a God and a Providence, and to this I have added, during my residence at Birmingham, a second part, in defence of the evidences of Christianity. . . .I can truly say, that the greatest satisfaction I receive from the success of my philosophical pursuits, arises from the weight it may give to attempts to defend Christianity, to free it from those corruptions which prevent its reception with philosophical and thinking persons, whose influence with the vulgar and unthinking is very great.[12]

In connection with American reactions to Priestley's religion we may single out what he says about Benjamin Franklin. Priestley was somewhat distressed to discover that a man of such "general good character and great influence should have been an unbeliever in Christianity, and also have done so much as he did to make others unbelievers."[13] At Franklin's request, Priestley recommended some readings on Christianity, but the American war broke out soon thereafter, and apparently there was no later opportunity for the two men to discuss such matters.

Active though he was in science during these free years from 1773 to 1780, Priestley nevertheless was extraordinarily productive in other ways as well. He says in his *Memoirs:* "Notwithstanding the attention that I gave to philosophy in this situation, I did not discontinue my other studies, especially in theology and metaphysics."[14] In 1777, while in the employ of Lord Shelburne, Priestley published his *Disquisitions Relating to Matter and Spirit.*[15] This work contains the clearest explicit statement of Priestley's scientific materialism in relation to his views on revelation, and forms the basis for many of his subsequent theological deliberations. It is appropriate to examine its thesis in some detail.

The circumstances of writing the *Disquisitions,* Priestley says in his *Memoirs,* were associated with the study and extension of David Hartley's philosophy. His own ideas were spelled out in 1775 in a treatise entitled *Hartley's Theory of the Human Mind, on the Principle of Association of Ideas: with Essays Relating to the Subject of it.* Concerning that work, Priestley wrote:

> I expressed some doubt of the immateriality of the sentient principle in man; and the outcry that was made on what I casually expressed on that subject can hardly be imagined. In all the newspapers, and most of the periodical publications, I was represented as an unbeliever in revelation, and no better than an Atheist.
>
> This led me to give the closest attention to the subject, and the consequence was the firmest persuasion that man is wholly material, and that our only prospect of immortality is from the Christian doctrine of a resurrection. I therefore digested my thoughts on the subject, and published my "Disquisitions

relating to Matter and Spirit:'' also the subjects of Socinianism and Necessity, being nearly connected with the doctrine of the materiality of man, I advanced several considerations from the state of opinions in ancient times in favour of the former; and in a separate volume, discussed more at large what related to the later. . . .[16]

What Priestley had to say about the relation of matter to spirit was illuminating, controversial, heretical, and, as he would have it, biblically sound. He approached the subject as follows:

It has generally been supposed that there are *two distinct kinds of substance* in human nature, and they have been distinguished by the terms *matter* and *spirit*. The former of these has been said to be possessed of the property of *extension,* viz. of length, breadth and thickness, and also of *solidity* or *impenetrability*, but it is said to be naturally destitute of all powers whatever. The latter has of late been defined to be a substance entirely *destitute of all extension,* or *relation to space*, so as to have no property in common with matter; and therefore to be properly *immaterial*, but to be possessed of the powers of *perception, intelligence* and *self-motion*.

Matter is that kind of substance of which our bodies are composed, whereas the principle of perception and thought belonging to us is said to reside in a *spirit*, or immaterial principle, intimately united to the body; while the higher orders of intelligent beings, and especially the Divine Being, are said to be purely immaterial.

It is maintained, in this treatise, that neither *matter* nor *spirit* (meaning by the latter the subject of sense and thought) correspond to the definitions above-mentioned. For, that matter is not that *inert* substance that it has been supposed to be; that *powers of attraction or repulsion* are necessary to its very being, and that no part of it appears to be *impenetrable* to other parts. I therefore define it to be a substance possessed of the property of *extension*, and of *powers of attraction or repulsion*. And since it has never yet been asserted, that the powers of *sensation and thought* are incompatible with these, (*solidity, or impenetrability* only, having been thought to be repugnant to them,) I therefore maintain, that we have no reason to suppose that there are in man two substances so distinct from each other as have been represented.[17]

For Priestley it was "both absurd and *modern*" to maintain that "two substances that have no common property" are "yet capable of *intimate connection* and *mutual action*."[18] To assert the existence of no material connections between two substances implied, he held, that there was no action between them. This was true simply because nonmaterial influences cannot act on material substances. Priestley saw it as modern perversion and as corruption of true religion to hold that substances can be conceived that have no extension or relation to place—a corruption, he said, that was "unknown both in the Scriptures and to all antiquity."[19] It was Priestley's intent to demonstrate that the modern matter-spirit dualistic philosophies and theologies and his own *"system of philosophy*, and the *true system of revelation,* have always been diametrically opposite, and hostile to each other; and that the latter can never be firmly established but upon the ruins of the former."[20]

Priestley's system was built upon a uniform conception of man that would encompass both body and mind. Man was taken to be wholly material. It was not, however, that mind was another form of substance distinct from the body. Rather, mind, or the principle of perception and thought, as Priestley conceived it, was the product of corporeal organization. "For, whatever matter may be," he says, "I think I have sufficiently proved that the human mind is nothing more than a modification of it."[21]

Priestley's masterialism was consistent with his anti-Trinitarian conception of Christ.

Again, that man is wholly material is eminently subservient to the doctrine of the *proper,* or *mere humanity* of Christ. For, if no man has a soul distinct from his body, Christ, who, in all other respects, appeared as man, could not have had a soul which had existed before his body; and the whole doctrine of the *pre-existence of souls* (of which the opinion of the pre-existence of Christ was a branch) will be effectually overturned. But I apprehend that, should I have failed in the proof of the materiality of man, arguments enow remain, independent of this, to prove the non-preexistence of Christ, and of this doc-

trine having been introduced into Christianity from the system
of Oriental philosophy.[22]

Likewise, the doctrine of necessity was seen by Priestley to be a
consequence of the conception of the materiality of man. This was
so because he equated mechanism with materialism, and
therefore argued that man's behavior necessarily is determined by
natural law. "I apprehend," he says, "that proof enough is advanced that every human volition is subject to certain fixed laws,
and that the pretended *self-determining* power is altogether
imaginary and impossible."[23]

Priestley concludes that materialism, Socinianism (anti-Trini-
tarianism), and philosophical necessity (mechanical determinism)
"are equally parts of *one system*, being equally founded on just
observations of nature, and fair deductions from the
Scriptures."[24] Having convinced himself, at least to his own satisfaction, that the phenomena associated with so-called "mind" or
"spirit," are adequately encompassed by natural law, Priestley
takes hold of the other end of the matter-spirit problem in order to
show that so-called "matter" possesses the properties and
powers attributed to "mind" or "spirit." Matter, too, has
powers. Take, for example, its property of impenetrability. Is this
due to resistance of anything material or solid? No! It is due to a
power of repulsion acting at a distance.

Priestley finds evidence for this assertion in the observation of
the resistance to the near approach of electrified bodies. He argues
that attractive forces, and not material solidity, are the cause of
the cohesion and thermal expansion of matter. "All the
phenomena of *light*," he remarks, "are most remarkably unfavourable to the hypothesis of the solidity or impenetrability of
matter."[25]

Consequently, the supposition of the *solidity* or *impenetrability* of matter, derived solely from the consideration of the
resistance of the solid parts of bodies. . .appears to be destitute
of all support whatever. The hypothesis was suggested by a

mere fallacy, and therefore ought to be discarded now that the fallacy is discovered.

It will be said, that if matter be not solid, or impenetrable substance, *what is it?* I answer, with respect to this, as I should with respect to any other substance, that it is possessed of such properties, and such only, as the actual well-examined *appearances* prove it to be possessed of. That it is possessed of powers of attraction and repulsion, and of several spheres of them, one within another, I know, because appearances cannot be explained without supposing them; but that there is anything in, or belonging to matter, capable of resistance, besides those powers of repulsion, does not appear from any phenomena that we are yet acquainted with, and, therefore, as a philosopher, I am not authorized to conclude that any such thing exists. On the contrary, I am obliged to deny that matter has such a property.[26]

In his *Disquisitions Relating to Matter and Spirit* Priestley further conjectures that man's seat of thought, his faculty of thinking, is a property inherent in the substance of his nervous system or his brain. He puts it as follows:

There is no instance of any man retaining the faculty of thinking, when his brain was destroyed; and whenever that faculty is impeded, or injured, there is sufficient reason to believe that the brain is disordered in proportion, and therefore we are necessarily led to consider the latter as the seat of the former.

Moreover, as the faculty of thinking in general ripens and comes to maturity with the body, it is also observed to decay with it; and if, in some cases, the mental faculties continue vigorous when the body in general is enfeebled, it is evidently because in those particular cases, the *brain* is not much affected by the general cause of weakness. But on the other hand, if the brain alone be affected, as by a blow on the head, by actual pressure within the skull, by sleep, or by inflammation, the mental faculties are universally affected in proportion.

Likewise, as the mind is affected in consequence of the affections of the body and brain, so the body is liable to be reciprocally affected by the affections of the mind, as is evident in the visible effects of all strong passions, hope or fear, love or anger, joy or sorrow, exultation or despair. These are certainly irrefragable arguments, that it is properly no other than *one and the same thing* that is subject to these affections, and that they are necessarily dependent upon one another.[27]

Priestley believed that his materialistic monism helped him to "get rid of all the embarrassment attending the doctrine of the soul." For, he says, man is "*one being, composed of one kind of substance, made of the dust of the earth*. . .[and] when he dies, he, of course, ceases to think."[28] Death, however, does not close the books on man's existence. Priestley firmly believed in the bodily resurrection, or, more correctly, in a matter-spirit resurrection. We must remember that matter and spirit were for Priestley a unity such that one cannot exist without the other.

At the resurrection, he says, when man's sleeping dust shall be reanimated, his power of thinking and his consciousness will be restored to him.

This system gives a real value to the doctrine of a *resurrection from the dead*, which is peculiar to revelation, on which alone the sacred writers build all our hope of a future life, and it explains the uniform language of the Scriptures, which speak of one day of judgement for all mankind, and represent all the rewards of virtue, and all the punishments of vice, as taking place at that awful day, and not before. This doctrine of a resurrection was laughed at by the conceited Athenians, and will always be the subject of ridicule to persons of a similar turn of mind; but it is abundantly confirmed to us by the well-attested resurrection of Jesus Christ, and the promises of the gospel, established on all the miraculous events by which the promulgation of Christianity was attended.[29]

If death is taken to consist of the putrefaction, or dispersion of parts, namely, the *de*composition of the body, then the resurrection corresponds to the *re*composition of the indestructible particles of matter. What God can decompose he can also recompose.

I doubt not but that, in the proper sense of the word, the *same body* that dies shall rise again, not with everything that is *adventitious* and *extraneous* (as all that we receive by nutrition), but with the same *stamina*, or those particles that really belonged to the *germ* of the organical body.[30]

Saint Paul compares the resurrection to the revival of a seed that has been sown in the earth and seemingly dies. This view is not entirely foreign to Priestley's interpretation.

For the *germ* does not die, and in our future transformation we may be as different from what we are in our present state, as the *plant* is from the *seed*, or the *butterfly* from the *egg*, and yet be essentially the same.[31]

In his *Doctrine of Philosophical necessity Illustrated* and published as an appendix to the *Disquisitions*, Priestley elucidated the doctrine that he had formulated much earlier. His principle of philosophical necessity was simply an extension of the idea that man, if wholly material, must be a mechanical being, such that the laws of nature and causality apply to all phenomena, so-called mental phenomena included.

As, therefore, every thing belonging to the doctrine of materialism is, in fact an argument for the doctrine of necessity, and, consequently, the doctrine of necessity is a direct inference from materialism, the defense of that inference would naturally accompany the proof of the proposition from which it was deduced.[32]

Priestley is all too aware, of course, that his philosophical doctrine of necessity, (his Necessarianism), resembles the Calvinistic doctrine of predestination. It is not feasible to discuss here all of the points of agreement and difference touched upon by Priestley. It may be sufficient, however, to give the gist of his reasoning. It goes as follows: Philosophical necessity implies causality. Existent causality relations, namely, the causal links that exist in the world, are established by the infinite wisdom of God. They are established in such a way as to terminate in the greatest good of the whole universe.[33] In this scheme, evils of all kinds are inseparable from God's overall plan. But, declares Priestley, no Necessarian, therefore, supposes, as the Calvinists do, that some persons will suffer eternal damnation while others reap eternal happiness. God is the author of all that is; and all that is, is an equally necessary part of the whole. However, the doctrine that God's divine plan relates sin, wrath, and redemption from sin for a select group of mankind to Jesus Christ as the second person in the Trinity, is decisively rejected by Priestley.

Comparing Calvinistic predestination with Necessarianism, Priestley asserts that the Calvinistic doctrine must lead to resignation by acceptance of whatever is, as inevitable. By contrast, Necessarianism points in the opposite direction, namely, to exertion, and striving, and to the deliberate cultivation of virtue, happiness, and success for the future. I confess that I do not follow completely the logic of Priestley's argument that attempts to correlate causality and Necessarianism.

Now, in comparing these two schemes, I can see no sort of resemblance, except that the future happiness or misery of all men is certainly fore-known and appointed by God. In all other respects they are most essentially different; and even where they agree in the *end*, the difference in the *manner* by which that end is accomplished is so very great, that the *influence* of the two systems on the minds of those that adopt and act upon them, is the reverse of one another, exceedingly favourable to virtue in the Necessarian, and as unfavourable to it in the Calvinist.

For, the essential difference between the two schemes is this: the Necessarian believes that his own dispositions and actions are the necessary and sole means of his present and future happiness; so that in the most proper sense of the words, it depends entirely upon *himself* whether he be virtuous or vicious, happy or miserable, just as much as it depends upon the farmer himself sowing his fields and weeding them, whether he will have a good crop; except that in favour of the doctrine of necessity where *morals* are concerned, his endeavours in the former case are much more certain in their effect than in the latter: which view of things cannot but operate to make him exert himself to the utmost in proportion to his regard for his own happiness, his success being certain in proportion to his exertion of himself. With this exertion he cannot miscarry, but without it he must, unless the laws of nature should change, be inevitably miserable. As far as any system of faith can induce men to cultivate virtuous principles and habits, this doctrine of necessity must do it.[34]

It is at this point, while discussing Priestley's deep-felt commitment to the doctrine of philosophical necessity, that I want to comment on his views regarding history, because I see that the two are closely related in his thought. Priestley was an inveterate historian—notably of science and of church history. He was a perceptive historian of science. He wrote an informative and influential history of electricity and a less successful history of optics. Fortunately, Priestley explicitly discusses his general views on the subject of history—for example, in his Lectures on *History and General Policy*. This is a work that was prepared at the Warrington Academy in 1761, but not put together for publication until 1781, or about four years after the publication of the *Disquisitions Relating to Matter and Spirit* that has just been discussed.

In these *Lectures on History* Priestley wrote:

In this view all true history has a capital advantage over every work of fiction. Works of fiction are not in their nature capable, in general, of any other uses than the authors of them had in view, which must necessarily be very limited; whereas true history, being an exhibition of the conduct of Divine Providence, in which every thing has, perhaps, infinite relations and uses, is an inexhaustible mine of the most valuable knowledge. Works of fiction resemble those machines which we contrive to illustrate the principles of philosophy, such as globes and orreries, the uses of which extend no further than the views of human ingenuity; whereas real history resembles the experiments made by the air pump, condensing engine and electrical machine, which exhibit the operations of nature, and the God of nature himself, whose works are the noblest subject of contemplation to the human mind, and are the groundwork and materials of the most extensive and useful theories.[35]

It was history that Priestley put to work in his own scholarly writings ''to free the mind from many foolish prejudices'' and particularly to avoid an ''unreasonable partiality'' for ones own country.[36] It is plausible to conjecture that in emphasizing history so keenly Priestley was emulating the strong historical bent of his intellectual mentor, Isaac Newton. History, Priestley felt, ''exhibits the conduct of Divine Providence, and points out the hand of God in the affairs of men.''[37] Here we see that his God is both the God of creation and the God of design.

Also, as nothing was *made*, so nothing can *come to pass*, without the knowledge, the appointment, or permission of God. Something, therefore, is intended by every thing that *happens*, as well as by everything that is *made*. But in little things a design is not so apparent as in greater and more striking things. Though, therefore, the hand of God be really in every thing that happens, and that is recorded in history, our attention is more forcibly drawn to it in great events, and especially in things which happen in a manner unexpected by us: in events in which the hand of man is least seen, the hand of God is most easily seen and acknowledged; though, in fact, it is equally concerned in every thing; men and their schemes and exploits being only instruments in his hand, employed as the most fit means to execute his purposes.[38]

Since, therefore, all that happens in history happens in accord with Divine Providence, it is of crucial importance to study history as a source of knowledge for *what is*. Thus will history ''throw an agreeable light upon [even] the most gloomy and disgusting parts of it.''

With a view to this, the most disagreeable objects in history will bear to be looked upon with satisfaction. And could we see every event in all its connexions and most distant influences, we should no doubt perfectly acquiesce in every thing that comes to pass under the government of God; in seeing that all evils lead to, and terminate in a greater good. But in many cases we see events which give us pain at first sight, and which occasion much regret and disappointment to those who give more scope to their passions than to their reflection while they are reading; which, nevertheless, if we look no further than the next and immediate consequences, we shall be thoroughly satisfied and pleased with.[39]

He adds: "These obvious remarks I mention here, to show the necessity of thought and *reflection* in reading history."[40]

One recognizes the same emphasis in a much earlier work, namely, in Priestley's *History and Present State of Electricity* of 1767:

An attention, indeed, to the conduct of divine Providence, which is ever bringing good out of evil, and gradually conducting things to a more perfect and glorious state, tends to throw a more agreeable light on the more gloomy parts of history, but it requires great strength of mind to comprehend those views; and, after all, the feelings of the heart too often overpower the conclusions of the head.[41]

Even more explicit, in its reference to Necessarianism is the following reflection:

A philosopher ought to be something greater, and better than another man. The contemplation of the works of God should give a sublimity to his virtue, should expand his benevolence, extinguish everything mean, base, and selfish in his nature, give a dignity to all his sentiments, and teach him to aspire to the moral perfections of the great author of all things. What great and exalted beings would philosophers be, would they let the objects about which they are conversant have their proper moral effect upon their minds! A life spent in the contemplation of the productions of divine power, wisdom, and goodness, would be a life of devotion. The more we see of the wonderful structure of the world, and of the laws of nature, the more clearly do we comprehend their admirable uses, to make all the percipient creation happy, a sentiment which cannot but fill the heart with unbounded love, gratitude, and joy.

Even every thing painful and disagreeable in the world appears to a philosopher, upon a more attentive examination, to be excellently provided, as a remedy of some greater inconvenience, or a necessary means of a much greater happiness; so that, from this elevated point of view, he sees all temporary evils and inconveniences to vanish, in the glorious prospect of the greater good to which they are subservient. Hence he is able to venerate and rejoice in God, not only in the bright sunshine, but also in the darkest shades of nature, whereas vulgar minds are apt to be disconcerted with the appearance of evil.[42]

Priestley's fourth pastorate at New Meeting, Birmingham, began in 1780 as the happiest event of his life but ended on Bastille Day, 14 July 1791, with the "Church-King" riots. The years in Birmingham were rich with philosophy and theology through associations with members of the Lunar Society and with congenial theologians of substance and true Christian temper. Concerning the Birmingham congregation Priestley wrote: "[I] introduced the custom of expounding the Scriptures as I read them."[43]

Apart from the *Disquisitions Relating to Matter and Spirit*, the most important work for understanding the underlying motives of Priestley's theology is his two-volume *History of the Corruptions of Christianity* published in 1782 while ministering to the Birmingham congregation. This work, devastating in its critique of most of the current Christian doctrines, was nevertheless warm and firm and genuine. It was, in fact, passionate in its religious fervency and defense of Christianity. The *Corruptions of Christianity* was dedicated to Rev. Theophilus Lindsay who had seceded from the Church of England, and in 1774 had opened the first Unitarian church in London. Together with Priestley, he was the most outstanding early leader of British Unitarianism. Priestley's dedicatory statement to Lindsay ends as follows:

> Let these views brighten the evening of our lives, that *evening*, which will be enjoyed with more satisfaction, in proportion as the *day* shall have been laboriously and well spent. Let us, then, without reluctance, submit to that temporary rest in the grave, which our wise Creator has thought proper to appoint for all the human race, our Saviour himself not wholly excepted: anticipating with joy the glorious *morning of the resurrection,* when we shall meet that Saviour, whose precepts we have obeyed, whose spirit we have breathed, whose religion we have defended, whose *cup* also we may, in some measure have drank of, and whose honours we have asserted without making them to interfere with those of *his Father and our Father, of his God and our God*, that supreme, that great and awful Being, to whose will he was always most perfectly submissive, and for whose unrivalled prerogative he always shewed the most ardent zeal.

With the truest affection,
I am,
Dear friend,
Your brother,
In the faith and hope of the gospel,
J. Priestley
Birmingham, Nov. 1782[44]

Among Priestley's writings, *The Corruptions of Christianity* undoubtedly achieved the greatest notoriety primarily because of his attack upon most of the fundamental doctrines that were held at the time by the established churches. The plan of the work was to uncover, by means of a historical analysis, the true, original, and primitive context of Christianity. In this way Priestley hoped to demonstrate that most contemporary orthodox views had been corrupted. In the end Priestley deemed to have shown, historically, from the original sources, the reprehensible, foreign, unfounded nature of the Trinity, the Virgin Birth, original sin, predestination, the vicarious atonement, and the plenary inspiration of the Scriptures.

Accordingly, the original highly prized and most valuable gifts of God to man were interpreted by Priestley to have been transformed within hostile quarters into the mischievous corrupted consequences of modern religion. Priestley felt that critics of the religion of Christianity, like Edward Gibbon in his *Decline and Fall of the Roman Empire*, had based their estimates of Christianity on its corruptions rather than upon its original, pure, genuine, rational form.[45] Now was the time, Priestley urged, to take advantage of the knowledge gleaned from historical researches to purge religion of all that had debased it and thus reestablish the pure revealed Christianity. Since God had permitted the corruption of Christianity to take place, for the best of purposes (Priestley's Necessarianism is shining through here), so God could now permit a reformation to occur. Thus, in time, good would result from evil. Priestley saw himself, here as elsewhere, performing the role of a messenger carrying out God's plan; thus taking advantage of a crisis (in corruption) to call attention to primitive Christianity, the return of which Priestley believed was not too distant.

> In the prospect of this great and glorious event I rejoice; and I wish to contribute a little towards hastening its approach, both by unfolding the history of Christianity, with all the corruptions of it, and submitting to the most rigid examination whatever I think to be really a part of it. To this, all the friends of genuine Christianity will cheerfully say, Amen.[46]

The first corruption of Christianity exposed by Priestley was the divinity of Christ. According to Scripture, Jesus was seen to be a *man* approved by God, by wonders and signs which God did by Him (*Acts 2:22*).[47] There was one God, and one mediator between God and men, the *man* Christ Jesus (*I Timothy 25*).[48]

[The Apostle Paul] does not say the *God*, the *God-man*, or the *super-angelic being,* but simply *the man* Christ Jesus; and nothing can be alleged from the New Testament in favour of any higher nature of Christ, except a few passages interpreted without any regard to the context, or the modes of speech and opinions of the times in which the books were written, and in such a manner, in other respects, as would authorize our proving any doctrine whatever from them.[49]

Thus the divinity of Christ was seen by Priestley to infringe upon the supremacy of God the Father. Jesus is a man, created, and not preexistent.

The second corruption, the modern doctrine of the atonement, flows from the first:

It is said that sin, as an offense against an *infinite Being*, requires an *infinite satisfaction*, which can only be made by an *infinite person,* that is, one who is no less than God himself. Christ, therefore, in order to make this infinite satisfaction for the sins of men, must himself be God, equal to the Father. The justice of God being now fully satisfied by the death of Christ, the sinner is acquitted. Moreover, as the sins of men have been thus imputed to Christ, his righteousness is, on the other hand, imputed to them; and thus they are accepted of God, not on account of what they have done themselves, but for what Christ had done for them.[50]

This doctrine, as Priestley saw it, is a gross misrepresentation, and a corruption in reasoning that has no basis in Scripture. Rather, it is a "disfiguring and depraving" departure "from the primitive and genuine doctrine of Christianity."[51]

The third corruption included in Priestley's critique was belief in the Virgin Birth of the Saviour—an idolatry that Priestley believed had generated the superstitious respect for relics, pictures, and images.[52] It eventually would lead, he suggested, to the deification of Mary. The manner in which Priestley proceeded to construct his arguments in regard to his conception of the distortions that lead to belief in the Virgin Birth are outlined in his *Corruptions of Christianity*, but similar views are explored yet more pointedly in still another treatise published several years later, in 1786, while he lived in Birmingham. It was the work in which he asserted: "[I] scrupled not to declare myself a *Materialist.*"[53] The title of this volume is: *An History of Early Opinions Concerning Jesus Christ, Compiled from Original Writers, Proving that the Christian was at First Unitarian.* "This work," he wrote in his *Memoirs,* "has brought me more antagonists, and I now write a pamphlet annually in defense of the Unitarian doctrine against all my opponents."[54]

One can examine, from this volume, Priestley's interpretation of *how* the Virgin Birth, or the doctrine of miraculous conception, entered as a corrupt doctrine into Christianity:

> The Scriptures. . .were written without any particular inspiration, by men who wrote according to the best of their knowledge, and who from their circumstances could not be mistaken with respect to the *greater facts*, of which they were proper *witnesses,* but (like other men, subject to prejudice) might be liable to adopt a hasty and ill-grounded opinion concerning things which did not fall within the compass of their own knowledge, and which had no connexion with anything that did so: and such I hold the miraculous conception to be. We ought all of us, therefore, to consider ourselves as fully at liberty to examine with the greatest rigour, both the *reasonings* of the writers, and the *facts* of which we find any account in their writings: that, judging by the rules of just criticism, we may distinguish what may be depended upon, from what may not."[55]

One notes that Priestley does not reject all miracles out of hand, but only such as may not "be depended upon." What criterion, one may inquire, did Priestley employ for distinguishing dependable or trustworthy miracles from untrustworthy miracles? His criterion was a two-sided one that sought to search out: (1) the importance or function of the miraculous event; and

(2) the strength of the historical evidence to support that event.

As the former, Priestley suggests, for example, that *how* Christ came into the world is unimportant and shows no advantage to the great object of his mission. What counts as important is "what he taught when he was in it, and what he did and suffered, as a proof of the authority by which he taught."[56] Rejecting the Virgin Birth as answering to no advantage, Priestley went one step further to emphasize its demerits:

> A *priori*, we should rather have thought. . .that there would have been a greater propriety in. . .[Christ's] being, in this as well as in all other respects, what other men are. For then, having had no natural advantage over us, his resurrection would have been calculated to give us the greater assurance of our own. Whereas, his coming into the world in a manner so very different from that of other men, might create a suspicion that there was some other essential difference between him and other men; and, therefore, that his nature might be subject to other laws than those of ours.[57]

Thus Priestley saw that the miraculous circumstances of Christ's birth "can only serve to puzzle, to amaze, and confound men; but [that] they have no tendency to mend the heart or the life."[58]

To put Priestley's views within a broader perspective, we recognize that he was ready to reject all so-called miracles that serve no purpose in the history of Christianity. While he rejected the miraculous conception of Christ, he did not reject Christ's resurrection. He also accepted Luke's account of the raising from the dead, of the widow's son, because it took place in the presence of thousands of witnesses (*Luke 7:11-17)*). By contrast he rejected the miraculous conception of Christ because there were no witnesses and because he felt that this miracle answered no Christian purpose whatsoever.

> The evidence for the miraculous conception, and that for the public life, miracles, death, and resurrection of Christ are exceedingly different; so that a total failure in the evidence for the one, will not affect the credibility of the other.[59]

Alleged miracles that are potentially purposeful—that serve some theological function in God's plan for man—must still, according to Priestley, be judged as to their credibility. He means, of course, historical credibility and not scientific credibility. As far as I know, scientific credibility does not enter into Priestley's discussion on this subject, except that he mentioned that the less reason there is to expect any particular event, the stronger should be the historical evidence required to validate it. Miracles, therefore, will require more evidence than ''notions of inspiration''; they will require very strong historical evidence:

> Setting aside all notions of *inspiration,* we should judge of the gospel history as we do of any other. . . .Making myself, therefore, perfectly easy as to all the possible consequences of this discussion, I shall, with perfect freedom, consider the evidence for the miraculous conception as an *article of history*, and shall, with as much care as I can, state the arguments for and against it.[60]

On the question of scriptural evidence for historically recorded events, including miracles, Priestley had something to say that foreshadowed the philological, historical, and theological thrust of the higher biblical criticism of the nineteenth century. Like David F. Strauss and Ludwig Feuerbach, for example, Priestley emphasized that the quantity and verity of evidence from Scripture must be evaluated, like any other historical document, without regard to alleged inspiration. He puts it this way:

> The observation which I would now make, and which I wish to impress upon my reader, is this; that fully to establish the credibility of any fact, it must not only be recorded by contemporary historians, but it must also appear not to have been contradicted by those who were contemporary with the historians, and who may be supposed to have been as good judges as the historians themselves. Still less will the single circumstance of an event being recorded by contemporary historians, avail to establish the credit of it, if it appear not to have been believed

by those who may be supposed to have been favourably inclined to the belief of it, and to have wished it to be true.[61]

Priestley also argued against the miraculous conception on the basis of evidence derived from the history of the early Christians:

> There is sufficient reason to think, that the great body of Jewish Christians, who were contemporary with the apostles, did not believe it. It was probably a long time before it gained any credit at all with any of their posterity, and it is probable that it never did so with the generality of them. It is certain that some very learned persons, and therefore, probably the most inquisitive among them, and who wrote expressly on the subject, never believed it.[62]

Likewise, he suggested that the Gospels themselves provided additional evidence to support his views:

> In comparing the four Gospels, we cannot but be struck with the remarkable difference between those of *Matthew* and *Luke,* and those of *Mark* and *John,* in this respect; neither of the latter giving the least hint of a miraculous conception. And yet it might well be thought that, if any part of the history required to be particularly authenticated, by the testimony of different historians, it was this; and many things of far less consequence are recorded by them all, and very circumstantially.[63]

Prior to 1791 Priestley was mostly engrossed in experimenting, in writing, and in preaching. To be sure, almost everything he wrote generated controversy in one quarter or another. But there is not a smidgen of evidence to suggest that he ever sought to stonewall himself into his study or laboratory in order to avoid public attack. Nor can one discern any loss of confidence, on his part, in his conceived mission to be a servant to persons of all beliefs or in his conviction of the historical and theologically uncorrupted Jesus Christ of the Scriptures. The serenity of Priestley's life was profoundly but only temporarily disturbed on Bastille day in 1791 when the mob burned his home and the meeting house in which he preached. His library, apparatus and belongings were demolished. Shortly thereafter he took his fifth pastorate in the borough of Hackney outside of London.

On the whole, I spent my time even more happily at Hackney than ever I had done before, having every advantage for my philosophical and theological studies, in some respect superior to what I enjoyed at Birmingham. . .Never, on this side the grave, do I expect to enjoy myself so much. . .conversing. . .on theological and other subjects. . . .

I found, however, my society much restricted with respect to my philosophical acquaintance, most of the members of the Royal Society shunning me on account of my religious or political opinions, so that I at length withdrew myself from them, and gave my reasons for so doing in the preface to my "Observations and Experiments on the Generation of Air from Water," which I published at Hackney; for, with the assistance of my friends, I had in a great measure replaced my apparatus, and had resumed my experiments, though after the loss of nearly two years.

Living in the neighborhood of the New College, I voluntarily undertook to deliver lectures to the pupils on the subject of "History and General Policy," which I had composed at Warrington, and also on "Experimental Philosophy, particularly including Chemistry," the "Heads" of which I drew up for this purpose, and afterwards published. In being useful to this institution, I found a source of considerable satisfaction to myself. Indeed, I have always had a high degree of enjoyment in lecturing to young persons, though more on theological subjects than on any other.[64]

Priestley valued highly the reception and pecuniary assistance of the young persons from his Hackney congregation. I think it fair to say that Priestley loved science and experimental work, that he was a theologian at heart, but that the Christian ministry was where he felt the strongest urge to serve in an active way. Indeed, he never lost sight of his local calling as a Christian minister even while hoping to bring to a wider audience the merits of his own Christian convictions. Thus, recognizing the

high position that he held in France, because of his pro-
revolutionary views (politically speaking) Priestley published in
1793, before he left London, his *Letters to the Philosophers and
Politicians of France on the Subject of Religion.* The light in
which he then stood in that country gave him some advantage, he
thought, in attempts to reinforce the evidence of natural and
revealed religion.

Over the thirty-nine years that bridge the period of the completion of his formal studies at Daventry and his move to
America, Priestley held five different pastorates for a total of
twenty-six years. For the remaining seven of those thirteen years
he was a tutor at the Academy in Warrington where he preached,
on the side, as a dissenting minister.

Concerning the move to America Priestley wrote in 1795:

> When I wrote the preceding part of these Memoirs, [while
> still in Birmingham] I was happy, as must have appeared in the
> course of them, in the prospect of spending the remainder of
> my life at Birmingham, where I had every advantage for pur-
> suing my studies, both philosophical and theological; but it
> pleased the Sovereign Disposer of all things to appoint for me
> other removals, and the manner in which they were brought
> about was more painful to me than the removals themselves. I
> am far, however, from questioning the wisdom or the goodness
> of the appointments, respecting myself or others.[65]

In Northumberland Priestley continued his defences of Unitarianism and his rectification of the misapprehensions of ecclesti-
cal historians concerning early opinions about Jesus. Even then,
at the age of sixty-one, he had not exhausted what he had wanted
to say in chemistry, theology, or anything else. During the last
decade of his life in America, he completed a six-volume *General
History of the Christian Church.* The dedicatory preface to
Thomas Jefferson, president of the United States, sang the praises
of America as the land of freedom. In America, he wrote, ''the
profession and practice of religion is as free as that of philosophy
or medicine.''[66]

Priestley's *General History* covered much of the same ground as his earlier writings—primarily that Christianity had been corrupted and perverted. Rationality, intelligibility, and simplicity had been neglected. The original biblical doctrine of one God, he believed, had given way to three separate deities, and was then followed by hundreds of subordinate ones:

> By this means we see how a just and merciful God, freely pardoning all sins that are repented of and forsaken, who expresses the most earnest desire that all would repent and live, came to be regarded as the most unreasonable of tyrants: not only requiring an infinite satisfaction for the slightest offenses, but dooming the greater part of his creatures to everlasting torments; a catastrophe foreseen, and intended by him before they were born."[67]

The historically simple and meaningful profession of religion by baptism had come "to be considered as actually of itself washing away sin, and a passport for a child to the happiness of heaven, which, without that ceremony, would have gone to hell."[68] To the practice of the partaking of bread, merely in remembrance of Christ, had been grafted the doctrine of transubstantiation and the complex ceremonies of the Mass.

> What an immense distance there is between a primitive Christian minister, the true servant of the servants of God, and him who, retaining that title, assumed all power in heaven and earth; making kings and emperors hold up his train when he walked in procession, and hold his stirrups and bridle when he mounted his horse.[69]

Consistent with Priestley's Necessarianism was his open-ended, optimism for the Christianity of the future. This is a dominant feature of Priestley's historically contingent theology in general; and it was explored in some depth in his *General History of the Christian Church:*

Hence we may safely conclude, that this natural process, now happily commenced, will proceed till every remaining corruption of Christianity be removed, and nothing will be found in it that any unbeliever, any Jew, or Mahometan, can reasonably object to. And since whatever is true and right will finally prevail, that is, when sufficient time has been given to the exhibition of it, rational Christianity will, in due time, be the religion of the world.[70]

As Priestley saw it, the natural process of history would run its course in such a way as eventually to draw all men to the Saviour, Jesus Christ. He meant by "all" to include obstinate and incredulous "Mahometans," Jews, skeptics, and unbelievers. Indeed, he welcomed their disapprobation toward Christianity as an intrinsic part of God's overall plan. For he felt that by raising objections to Christianity and thus purging religion "from everything that is offensive to right reason" the nonbelievers were, in fact "preparing the way for their own conversion."[71] Thus, the success of Christianity was assumed to be historically inevitable.

The very last scientific work that Priestley wrote while in Northumberland, Pennsylvania, was his *Doctrine of Phlogiston Established and that of the Composition of Water Refuted.* In the face of opposition from virtually the whole chemical community Priestley continued to hold fast to the view that water is an element and that phlogiston is liberated in combustion. At the head of this chemical treatise of 1800 stands a kind of dissenter's confession of faith that demonstrates how decisively Priestley placed matters of religion above those of science.

My philosophical friends must excuse me, if, without neglecting natural science, I give a decided preference to theological studies; and if here, as in Europe, I give the greatest part of my time to them. They are, unquestionably, of unspeakably more importance to men, as beings destined for immortality; and I apply myself with so great satisfaction to the study of nature, not so much on account of the advantage we derive from it at present, though this is very considerable, as from its being a delightful field of speculation, barely opening to us here, and to be resumed with far greater advantage in a future state.

No discovery in philosophy [read science] bears any proportion in real value to that of *bringing life and immortality to light,* which is completely effected in the gospel, and nowhere else. None of our experiments, or observations on the course of nature, could have given us the least glimpse of this.[72]

Chemist, political rebel, educator, historian, natural philosopher that he was, I see the juncture of Priestley's intellectual and practical beliefs embedded in a theology that rests upon the solid evidence provided by history—as he read it. Nonconformist preacher-servant, skilled biblical polemicist, resolute and radically empiricist historian, Priestley was at one and the same time a devastating critic of current Christian doctrine and a zealous defender of the original, pure, genuine, revealed, primitive, rational Christianity. He recognized true, real history as the most transparent and elegant exhibition of the conduct of divine providence, and therefore of rational religion. It is accurate to say that he was a skilled, prolific, and imaginative experimentalist; but he was no less versatile and inventive as a theologian who held in his grasp a prodigious capacity and prowess for accommodation and change in matters of philosophy and religious doctrine.

All of Priestley's theological and extrascientific writings reveal the restless struggle of a scholar intent on recapturing a historically purer and more primitive revelation with the intent of integrating that true revealed religion with the scientific materialism of the age. To this end any kind of argument based on or leading to a dualism or bifurcation of matter and spirit, or of body and soul, was ruthlessly rejected. Joseph Priestley was truly a God-intoxicated materialist.

NOTES

1. Joseph Priestley, *The Theological and Miscellaneous Works of Joseph Priestley, LL.D., F.R.S. &c.* ed. John Towill Rutt, 25 vols. in 26 (London, 1817-31). Most of the quotations in this paper are taken from this collection and will be referred to as *Rutt.* Volume 1., part 1, contains *Memoirs and Correspondence, 1733-87.* Volume 1., part 2., contains *Life and Correspondence, 1787-1804.* Volumes 2 through 25 contain theological and miscellaneous writings.
2. *Rutt*, pt. 1:11.
3. *Defences of the History of the Corruptions of Christianity in reply to Dr. Horsley and Mr. Babcock,* (1786), *Rutt,* 18:37.
4. Rutt, 1, pt. 1:11.
5. Ibid., pp. 23-24.
6. Ibid., pp. 24-25.
7. Ibid., pp. 25-27.
8. Ibid., p. 40.
9. Ibid., p. 59.
10. Ibid., p. 76.
11. Ibid., p. 68.
12. Ibid., pp. 198-200.
13. Ibid., p. 212.
14. Ibid., p. 201.
15. The complete title of this work is *Disquisitions Relating to Matter and Spirit, to which is added the History of the Philosophical Doctrine concerning the Origin of the Soul, and the Nature of Matter: with its Influence on Christianity, especially with Respect to the Doctrine of the Preexistence of Christ* (London, 1777). *Rutt,* 3 contains the second "improved and enlarged" edition of 1782.
16. *Rutt,* 1, pt. 1:202-3.
17. *Disquisitions Relating to Matter and Spirit, Rutt, 3:218-19.*
18. Ibid., p. 219.
19. Ibid.
20. Ibid.
21. Ibid., p. 220.
22. Ibid.
23. Ibid.
24. Ibid.
25. Ibid., p. 228.
26. Ibid., p. 229.
27. Ibid., p. 244.
28. Ibid., p. 286.
29. Ibid., p. 276.
30. Ibid., p. 332.
31. Ibid.

32. *The Doctrine of Philosophical Necessity Illustrated, Rutt,* 3:453.
33. Bentham's ''greatest good for the greatest number'' is derived from Priestley's statement of this utilitarian principle.
34. Ibid., pp. 534-35.
35. *Lectures on History and General Policy, Rutt,* 24:27-28.
36. Ibid., p. 32.
37. Ibid., p. 44.
38. Ibid., p. 45.
39. Ibid., p. 47.
40. Ibid., p. 48.
41. *The History and Present State of Electricity with Original Experiments,* Preface to the first edition of 1767. Reprinted with an Introduction by Robert E. Schofield (New York, 1966). p. 3.
42. Ibid., pp. xxiii-xxiv.
43. *Rutt,* 1, pt. 1:339-40.
44. *An History of the Corruptions of Christianity, Rutt,* 5:6.
45. Ibid., pp. 480-94.
46. Ibid., p. 494.
47. Acts 2:11: ''Ye men of Israel, hear these words: Jesus of Nazareth, a man approved by God among you by miracles and wonders and signs, which God did by him in the midst of you, as ye yourselves also know.''
48. *1 Timothy* 2:5: ''For there is one God, and one mediator between God and men, the man Jesus Christ.''
49. *An History of the Corruptions. . . ., Rutt,* 5:14.
50. Ibid., p. 91-92.
51. Ibid., p. 92.
52. Ibid., pp. 180-216.
53. *An History of Early Opinions, Rutt,* 7:58.
54. *Rutt,* 1, pt. 1:341.
55. *An History of Early Opinions, Rutt.* 7:58-59.
56. Ibid., p. 61.
57. Ibid., p. 66.
58. Ibid., p. 61.
59. Ibid., p. 63.
60. Ibid., pp. 63-64.
61. Ibid., pp. 82-83.
62. Ibid., p. 84.
63. Ibid., p. 100.
64. *Rutt,* 1, pt. 2:119-20.
65. Ibid., p. 2.
66. *A General History of the Christian Church, From the Fall of the Western Empire to the Present Time, Rutt,* 9:5.
67. Ibid., 10:533.
68. Ibid., p. 533.
69. Ibid.

70. Ibid., p. 534.
71. Ibid., p. 535.
72. *The Doctrine of Phlogiston Established and that of the Composition of Water Refuted.* Preface (Northumberland, 1800).

2

Priestley and Lavoisier

AARON J. IHDE

University of Wisconsin, Madison

Although Joseph Priestley and Antoine Lavoisier met on only one occasion, their scientific careers were closely intertwined. Priestley discovered the gas that Lavoisier adopted as the central element in the new view of chemistry that he developed; nevertheless, Priestley was never able to bring himself to adopt the new chemistry of Lavoisier and in the last years of his life was occupied with the writing of tracts in opposition to the antiphlogiston point of view.

There has been frequent allusion in chemistry classrooms (and in the historical literature) to the irony that Priestley, the discoverer of oxygen and a man noted for his radical religious and social views, should have been unable to accept the new chemistry that Lavoisier created around oxygen. In reality the issue has become blurred with the passage of time, and this, coupled with constant classroom pressures to simplify for the sake of pedagogical convenience, has led to simplistic views that make Priestley appear like a feeble theorist at best and a stubborn conservative at worst. At the same time, Lavoisier is made to come off like an experimental genius and intellectual giant.

What are the facts? To what extent were both scientists creatures of their times, destined to see the same facts from a different vantage point? To what extent did they influence one another? To what extent did they understand one another? And to what extent may personal animosities have figured in their relationships? This paper is an effort to examine these questions.

Whoever makes an exploration of the careers of the two men within the context of their times is almost certain to come away with a profound respect for both as scientists. To both, science was a fascinating avocation to be pursued in those moments free from the work of theology and business. Although Priestley was the elder by a decade, their entrance into scientific studies was almost simultaneous. Lavoisier's career ended prematurely with his execution at age fifty-one; Priestley's career would extend another decade. However, spending the last decade of his life in America took him away from the mainstream of science and somewhat negated his influence. The interrelationships between the science of the two men can be separated into two questions: (1) What did Lavoisier know and when did he know it?, and (2) What did Priestley learn, and why didn't he believe it?

WHAT DID LAVOISIER KNOW (ABOUT OXYGEN) AND WHEN DID HE KNOW IT?

The only meeting of Priestley and Lavoisier took place in October 1774 when Priestley accompanied his patron, Lord Shelburne, on a continental trip, which included Paris. According to a later statement of Priestley,[1] he attended a meeting with Lavoisier and other French scientists at which he discussed an air produced from the red calx of mercury (HgO) by heating with a large lens. Priestley inferred that his remarks led Lavoisier to experiment with the gas produced from the red calx.

Although possibly piqued by Lavoisier's failure to call attention to his information, Priestley's case for recognition on this point is weak. At the time of the meeting Priestley himself failed to understand the nature of his gas. He looked upon it as "dephlogisticated nitrous air" (laughing gas or nitrous oxide, N_2O) a gas he had prepared from spirit of nitre (HNO_3) and studied earlier. When he encountered oxygen early in August 1774, Priestley made only superficial studies of it. He saw that it was not soluble in water and that it enhanced the flame of a candle, just as did dephlogisticated nitrous air. But he was puzzled that he could produce such a gas from *mercurius calcinatus per se* since this substance was prepared by direct heating of mercury. Could his material perhaps be *red precipitate?* The latter was customarily prepared by dissolving mercury in spirit of nitre, then precipitating the *red precipitate* by adding alkali. Priestley puzzled over why he might obtain "dephlogisticated nitrous air" from *mercurius calcinatus* when the latter had no prior association with nitre in the form of spirit of nitre. Therefore, the suspicion arose that his red substance might not be *mercurius calcinatus per se,* but *red precipitate* instead, thus accounting for the release of dephlogisticated nitrous air. However, in his August experiments he had also prepared the unique air from *red precipitate* and from red lead (Pb_3O_4). Before leaving Paris he would procure for further studies a sample of genuine *mercurius calcinatus per se* from Cadet de Gassicourt, a pharmacist of unquestioned skill and reliability.

The gas that Priestley described to Lavoisier and the assembled scientists in Paris was looked upon as "dephlogisticated nitrous air." Knowledge of it would be of no help to Lavoisier in his pursuit of an understanding of the processes of calcination and combustion. Although Lavoisier performed experiments with *mercurius calcinatus* in November, the experiments were inconclusive and were soon abandoned. It might of course be argued that Priestley's reference to the decomposition of the calx of mercury was of critical significance to Lavoisier. Such can hardly have been the case, except for recalling attention to experimental facts already available to Lavoisier.

In February 1774 the pharmacist Bayen had reported the conversion of calx of mercury to mercury by heating,[2] with the simultaneous release of a gaseous material assumed to be fixed air (CO_2).[3] The reports were published in Rozier's journal and can hardly have escaped Lavoisier's notice since he frequently used the same journal as a vehicle for rapid publication of his own studies. Similar information came to Lavoisier's attention on 3 September 1774 when Cadet de Gassicourt announced to the Académie des Sciences that *mercurius calcinatus per se* was reduced to mercury by mere heating, without benefit of a source of phlogiston such as charcoal. The information was confirmed on 13 November 1774 in a report to the Académie made by Sage, Brisson, and Lavoisier.[4]

Still another incident that would have made Lavoisier familiar with such information as was relayed to him by Priestley was a letter sent to him by Scheele on 30 September 1774.[5] Scheele's letter called attention to the preparation of a new gas that he would later call *Feuerluft*, prepared by heating carbonate of silver and absorbing the carbon dioxide in alkali. Scheele asked Lavoisier to perform the experiment with his superior burning glass and appraise him of the results. The Scheele letter was never referred to publicly by Lavoisier, yet there is evidence of its having reached him.[6] Although Scheele's interpretation of the new gas would ultimately be clothed in phlogistic interpretations, his factual description of the gas in the letter was clearer than that of Bayen at the time. Further, it added new evidence that a unique gas could be produced by heating a calx without charcoal.

There can be little quarrel with the position that although Priestley considered the October 1774 comments significant, they were of no unique value to Lavoisier. Lavoisier had no use for the information that ''dephlogisticated nitrous air'' might be produced by heating the red calx of mercury.[7]

By the following March both Lavoisier and Priestley were

arriving independently at a new understanding of the gas driven from red calx of mercury by heating. The previous November Priestley had prepared a new supply of air from the genuine *mercurius calcinatus per se* procured in Paris and extended his studies of its properties. He now saw that, not only did it augment the flame of a candle but it retained that capacity even after prolonged agitation with water. Genuine "dephlogisticated nitrous air" prepared from spirit of nitre, however, tended to lose its capacity to augment the candle flame after agitation with water.

On 1 March 1775 Priestley mixed air from the calx of mercury with nitrous air and observed that it became red and "diminished quite as much as common air."[8] This observation involving the nitrous air test was of critical importance in leading to a clearer understanding of the nature of the new gas.

Several years earlier, on 4 June 1772, Priestley had prepared "nitrous air" (nitric oxide, NO) by the action of spirit of nitre on mercury and other metals.[9] Study of the properties of the nitrous air revealed a failure to dissolve in water. The air, however, reacted easily with common air, giving reddish fumes which were readily soluble in water (with the formation of spirit of nitre).

Priestley took advantage of the reaction to devise a test for the "goodness of air."[10] Working with cylinders in the pneumatic trough he found that by pouring one measure of nitrous air into two measures of good quality common air, one saw evidence for reddish fumes that soon dissolved in the confining water. A residual volume of 1.8 measures of undissolved gas was left. When the same test was made on common air, which had been spoiled by either burning a candle therein or allowing an animal to breathe therein, the volume of undissolved gas was greater than 1.8 measures, frequently being more than two measures. Thus, Priestley had devised a quantitative test for measurement of quality of atmospheric air, a shrinkage to 1.8 volumes being representative of good common air; a residual volume greater than 1.8 volumes revealing a sample of common air that had been spoiled to a particular degree.

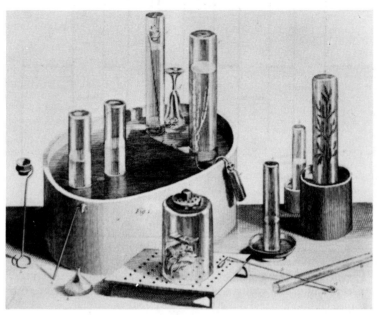

Apparatus used by Priestley for the study of gases. From Priestley, *Experiments and Observations on Different Kinds of Air*, vol. 1 (1774).

When Priestley renewed his studies of the gas from calx of mercury on 1 March 1775 he applied the nitrous air test to the new air, with the surprising observation that ''it was diminished quite as much as common air, and that the redness of the mixture was likewise equal to that of a similar mixture of nitrous and common air.''[11] It was at this point that he became persuaded that he was not dealing with ''dephlogisticated nitrous air'' but was studying a unique gas with the general characteristics of good common air but in a more accentuated form. Would it show similar characteristics when breathed?

On 8 March Priestley placed a mouse in a vessel containing two ounces of the new air from calx of mercury. The mouse was left in the vessel for a half hour. When removed, apparently dead,

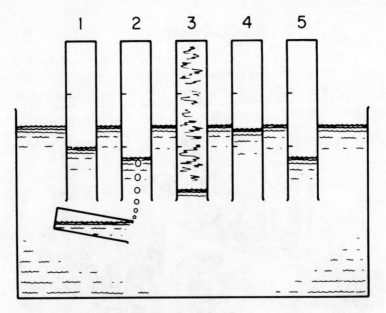

Priestley's "Nitrous Air Test for the Goodness of Air."

   1 represents two volumes of test gas (air) confined over water.

   2 represents one volume of nitrous air (NO) being added to the test gas.

   3 represents the added volume of nitrous air before the reddish fumes (NO_2) have dissolved to a significant degree in the confining water.

   4 represents a residual volume of 1.8 volumes after the red fumes have dissolved. This result is characteristic of the results with "good common air."

   5 represents a residual volume greater than two volumes after the red fumes have dissolved. Such a result is obtained from air that has been exhaled from the lungs or in which a candle flame has burned to the point of extinction.

and held near the fire it revived, presumably unharmed by the experiment. Prior experience with mice placed in the same volume of common air had been death within a quarter hour. At this point Priestley considered the air from calx of mercury to be at least as good as common air, but because of differences in individual mice it still did not occur to him that the prepared air might be better.

The next day he decided to try the nitrous air test on the residual gas from which the mouse had been removed in order to measure the degree of noxiousness caused by the respiration of the mouse. To his surprise, the gas tested better than common air! Had the gas been respired common air it would have been obviously noxious, according to past experience with the test.

After overnight reflection on the matter Priestley added another measure of nitrous air to the residual gas from the previous day's test and ". . .To my utter astonishment, [I] found that it was farther [sic] diminished to almost one half of its original quantity. I then put a third measure to it; but this did not diminish it any farther [sic]."[12]

Subsequent studies of the gas from calx of mercury persuaded him that mice lived appreciably longer in it. He further learned that two measures of the gas accepted four measures of nitrous air and that the gas from *red precipitate* showed the same behavior as that from *mercurius calcinatus per se*. It was now evident to him that the gas was not dephlogisticated nitrous air. It was a form of common air with a greatly enhanced capacity to support combustion and respiration. In fact, it was common air deprived of virtually all of its phlogiston and therefore unusually capable of participating in such chemical processes as involved the emission of phlogiston. For the gas he proposed the name "dephlogisticated air."[13] His experiments and conclusions were quickly communicated to the Royal Society in letters to Sir John Pringle (15 March and 24 May) and to Dr. Price (1 April).[14]

In summary, Priestley's discovery of dephlogisticated air dates from March 1775. He had first consciously prepared the gas on 1 August 1774 but confused it, on the basis of the properties then studied, with dephlogisticated nitrous air, first prepared in 1772. His work in March established its uniqueness on the basis of not only its superior capacity to support combustion (a characteristic held in common with dephlogisticated nitrous air) but its superior capacity to support respiration and to show a vastly greater shrinkage in the nitrous air test.

In the meantime, Lavoisier was pursuing similar studies. Between late February and mid-April 1775 he too was decomposing the red calx of mercury. But he was interested primarily in learning the possible role of the air in the formation of metal calxes. For nearly a decade his reading and experimentation were leading him to recognize that a combination with air was taking place during combustion and calcination. The calx of mercury afforded a unique opportunity to test the hypothesis. Earlier experiments involving the combustion of phosphorus and sulfur and the calcination of lead and tin had established the shrinkage of the air during the process (together with a gain in weight of the reacting substance). These reaction products, however, resisted efforts toward release of the combined air, except that the metal calxes could be converted to metal by heating with charcoal. Since the released air in such cases was fixed air, Lavoisier was at first inclined to believe that it was fixed air that combined with the metal and augmented the weight of the calx. The calx of mercury, however, could be converted to mercury by heating without the assistance of charcoal, hence it provided an opportunity to study the fixation and release of air during calcination and decomposition respectively.

Lavoisier's experiments during this period were summarized in a paper read before the Académie des Sciences on 26 April 1775 and commonly known as the ''Easter Memoir.'' It was published in Rozier's *Observationes sur la physique* in May.[15] He reported the results of two sets of experiments in which a definite quality of red calx of mercury was heated in a small retort [vessel] delivering into a tall bell jar filled with water for collection of the gases disengaged from the calx.

In the *first* experiment Lavoisier reported heating one *once* (30.58 grams) of calx mixed with 48 grains (2.6 g.) of powdered carbon. The calx was readily converted to mercury with the simultaneous evolution of 64 cubic *pouces* (1.27 liters) of air (without accounting for gas dissolved in the water in the bell jar). Tests on the gas showed that: (1) it dissolved in water during

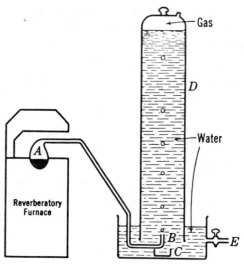

Lavoisier's Experiment dealing with the air evolved when the calx of mercury is heated.
James B. Conant, ed., *The Overthrow of the Phlogiston Theory*, Harvard University Press, Cambridge, 1950, copyright by the President and Fellows of Harvard College, with permission.

agitation, giving the water the acidic characteristic of well-known mineral waters; (2) it quickly asphyxiated animals placed in the gas; (3) it instantly extinguished flames of combustible substances; (4) it formed a precipitate with lime water; and (5) it combined readily with alkalies, both fixed and volatile, and reduced their causticity and converted them to crystallizable salts. These properties were those of fixed air (CO_2), obtained from all metallic calxes by addition of carbon, thus establishing *mercurius calcinatus per se* to be a true calx (a point which had been disputed as a result of its ability to decompose into mercury when heated without charcoal.).

In the *second* experiment Lavoisier reported heating one *once* of calx of mercury without charcoal in the same apparatus. It was necessary to heat to redness before decomposition took place but he then recovered 7 *gros*, 18 grains (27.72 g.) of mercury and 78 cubic *pouces* (1.55 l.) of air having a density similar to common air. Tests on this air revealed that: (1) it was not soluble in water even when agitated; (2) it failed to form a precipitate with lime water; (3) it failed to combine with fixed or volatile alkalies; (4) it did not diminish the causticity of alkalies; (5) it served anew for the calcination of metals; and (5) it was diminished like common air by a measure of nitrous air. Obviously, it showed none of the characteristics of fixed air.

Lavoisier commented that he was convinced that this latter air was ''not only common air, but that it was more respirable, more combustible, and consequently that it was even more pure than the air in which we live.''[16]

The memoir as publishesd in Rozier's journal soon came to the attention of Priestley who, in volume 2 of *Experiments and Observations on Different Kinds of Air*, would comment critically. Had Lavoisier simply tested the gas from calx of mercury with a second measure of nitrous air, and a third, he would have observed that the gas, far from being common air, was a dephlogisticated form of common air.[17]

Volume 2 of *Experiments and Observations* was printed in November 1775. Sheets reached Paris early in December and provided Lavoisier with the needed clue to enable him to piece together his puzzle. He was soon at work in the laboratory and came to recognize the uniqueness of Priestley's dephlogisticated air. His notebooks kept during 1776 and 1777 reveal that he repeated many of Priestley's experiments with care and understanding. For example, on 13 February 1776 he prepared ''1' air déphlogistique de M. Prisley'' [*sic*].[18] But he also extended Priestley's experiments in new directions, giving attention not only to the combination of dephlogisticated air with metals, but to the nature of the air remaining after a calcination was complete.

In April 1776 he calcined mercury by heating a weighed

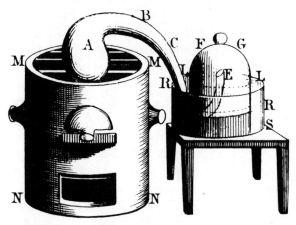

Lavoisier's Experiment on the Calcination of Mercury in Air. From *Oeuvres de Lavoisier*, J. B. Dumas, ed., 1862, vol. 1, plate 1.

sample of the metal for nearly two weeks in a retort which delivered into a bell jar placed in a trough containing mercury.

Here he could observe, much better than in earlier experiments on the calcination of tin and lead, the simultaneous formation of red calx and shrinkage of the air. The experiment, never fully described until publication of his textbook in 1789,[19] undoubtedly had a profound influence in the clarification of his thoughts. Measurements before and after heating revealed that the air was diminished by about one-sixth during calcination. Tests of the residual air showed that it did not precipitate lime water, hence could not be fixed air even though it extinguished candles and asphyxiated animals. He came to realize that combustion was partially absorption and partially vitiation of the air. He subsequently mixed five parts of such residual air with one part of dephlogisticated air to obtain a gas that supported the combustion of a candle about as well as ordinary air.

By April 1777 he had come to the conclusion that common air is a mixture of the "most respirable part" (Priestley's dephlogisticated air) with a portion left behind during calcination which he would soon call a *mofette*. Even before this he had concluded that during combustion and respiration carbonaceous matter combined with the ''eminently respirable air'' to form fixed air.[20]

By now (mid-1777) Lavoisier had moved far beyond Priestley's position, but under the stimulus of Priestley's experiments. Priestley would continue to hold a modification theory regarding the nature of common air—it might be badly phlogisticated (e.g., nitrogen), or quite lacking in phlogiston (e.g., dephlogisticated air), or show the characteristics usually associated with air. Lavoisier was now looking upon common air as a mixture, with one of the components directly involved in combustion, calcination, and respiration. That position was arrived at slowly. It was in a paper submitted on 5 September 1777 and read on 23 November 1779 dealing with ''eminently respirable air'' as an acidifying principle that the terms *principe acidifiant* or ''principe oxygine (Gr., *oxus* = acid; *gennao* = I beget) were introduced.[21]

In the meantime, Lavoisier was reworking the ''Easter Memoir'' in the light of his new understanding of the gas obtained from calx of mercury. The *Mémoires* of the French Academy were never published promptly after reading, the time lag frequently being up to three years. Thus, the volume for 1775 did not appear in print until 1778. It was Lavoisier's practice to seek prompt publication of his papers, utilizing Rozier's journal for the purpose. Since his ideas had frequently matured by the time the official *Mémoires* were published, he took advantage of the delay to incorporate changes into the official version. This was the case with the ''Easter Mémoire.''[22]

His changes in this paper were few and subtle. They went largely unnoticed in the nineteenth century since the later version was incorporated into the collected works prepared by Mme. Lavoisier as the *Mémoires de Chimie*[23] in 1805 and by J. B. Dumas in the *Oeuvres de Lavoisier*[24] in 1862. Only in recent decades, as the result of various studies, has it become general knowledge that two versions of several of the important papers exist—the paper as read, in Rozier's journal, and the paper as re-visited on the basis of new knowledge—in the *Mémoires* of the Académie.

Conant has very revealingly aligned changed portions of the Easter Memoir to bring out the variation in the two versions.[25] The list below shows one of these changes.

(1) that it was not susceptible to combination with water upon shaking;

(2) that it did not precipitate lime water;

(3) that it did not combine with fixed or volatile alkalis;

(4) that it did not at all diminish their caustic qualities;

(1) that it was not susceptible to combination with water upon shaking;

(2) that it did not precipitate lime water {*but only made it turbid to an almost imperceptible degree*};

(3) that it did not combine with fixed or volatile alkalis;

(4) that it did not at all diminish their caustic qualities;

[these first four tests were designed to show whether the gas was in whole or part "fixed air" as Bayen had reported; obviously it was not;]

(5) that it could be used again for the calcination of metals;

(6) that it was diminished like common air by an addition of a third of nitrous air;

(5) that it could be used again for the calcination of metals;

Comparison of Lavoisier's Summation of the Properties of the Air Removed from the Calx of Mercury by Heating. From James B. Conant, ed., *The Overthrow of the Phlogiston Theory*, Harvard University Press, Cambridge, 1950, copyright by the President and Fellows of Harvard College, with permission.

Here Lavoisier lists four tests designed to show that the gas is not fixed air. The items are identical except for an inconsequential observation in number 2. Number 5, revealing that the gas can be used again for calcination of metals, is the same. Number 6 is very revealing since, curiously, the observation on the nitrous air test is missing from the revised version. Why should it have been omitted in the revision? It is clearly related to Priestley's criticism in volume 2 of the *Experiments and Observations,* published in November 1775. It was this point that would lead Lavoisier to understand the uniqueness of the gas in the resolution of his problem. His notebooks carry experimental observations on the nitrous air test. Logical analysis and completeness of the record should have included revision of number 6, yet Lavoisier chose to omit the point entirely. What does the omission mean?

WHAT DID PRIESTLEY LEARN, AND WHY DIDN'T HE BELIEVE IT?

Before examining Priestley's rejection of Lavoisier's new chemistry, one should review what was involved. There has been a tendency to look upon Lavoisier's contribution as the rejection of phlogiston as the cause of combustion and calcination, with the substitution of a system in which oxygen of the air reacts with the combustible material to form oxides. While this is an important and clearly visible part of the new chemistry, it is only a segment of the whole system.

The new chemistry, as developed in journal publications in the seventies and eighties,[26] in the book on nomenclature reform,[27] in the *Traité élémentaire de chimie,*[28] and in the program of propaganda[29] included as a minimum, the following concepts: (1) Combustion and calcination involve combination with the basis of oxygen, the formation of oxides accounting for the weight gain of the metal on calcination; (2) Air is a mixture of azote and oxygen;

(3) Water is a compound of hydrogen and oxygen; (4) Caloric or heat substance, associated with the basis of oxygen, is released during combustion; (5) Combination with oxygen produces acids; (6) Matter is composed of simple bodies (elements), free or in combination. Simple bodies have never been simplified further by analysis (an operational definition); (7) Matter is conserved during chemical changes; (8) A new nomenclature expresses chemical composition.

Many commentators have failed to realize that Lavoisier's chemistry involved much more than abandonment of the subtle substance, phlogiston, and the introduction of oxygen into the combustion process. Had the matter been this simple and straightforward there would, perhaps, have been only a small impact on chemical thought.

First of all, the phlogiston concept had been a vague part of chemistry for something over a half century. Contrary to common belief nowadays, it had never been a well-defined, widely held hypothesis before it came under attack by Lavoisier. Chemists were inclined to use it or avoid it as they saw fit. For one thing, there was never any general agreement regarding the assumptions of the phlogiston theory. As the *terra pinguis* of Becher, it was a vague extension of sulfur in the three principles of the Paracelsians. As developed in the writings of Stahl early in the eighteenth century it took on the character of a subtle principle that when present in a body, caused the body to undergo combustion, the phlogiston escaping during the process. Although positions varied, phlogiston was never clearly equated with flame since charcoal glowed without flame and metals underwent calcination without flame.

In the writings of later commentators, the views of Stahl were frequently garbled and often extended. As a conveniently vague principle, phlogiston was used to explain not only chemical changes involving heat and light but those involving acidity, causticity, effervescence, color changes, and other phenomena. By 1770 it was many things to many men, and nothing to others.

The phlogiston that Lavoisier would soon attack was, in some respects, a concept of his own making. He would focus directly on a substance that, on escaping from a hot metal, would leave the resultant calx a heavier body.

Throughout his business and scientific career, Lavoisier would proceed on the philosophy that *outgo* must equal *income,* the principle being expressed somewhat obscurely in the *Traité* while discussing alcoholic fermentation,[30] and later to become known as the law of conservation of matter. Although only expressing the concept once, and then rather vaguely, Lavoisier carried out his studies as if *income* equals *outgo* was a matter of faith.

Many contemporary scientists, including Priestley, were less prone to place great faith in conservation laws, particularly when dealing with subtle phenomena such as electricity, light, heat, and phlogiston. The balance was not yet an instrument of ultimate recourse in the laboratory. Chemical science was still in a stage where much valuable understanding could be obtained by qualitative observation. In fact, had not Hales, a half-century earlier, carried out prodigious measurements on the quantity of air released by a variety of solids on heating, while missing almost entirely the qualitative differences in the airs liberated?[31] Hales would leave to posterity a mass of quantitative data of no scientific significance, while failing to understand the significance to science of the apparatus developed to carry out the measurements— the pneumatic trough.[32] Priestley, the qualitative scientist *par excellence,* would utilize that trough to recognize a whole host of new gases, while Lavoisier, of a more quantitative bent, would adapt the trough to new uses toward the creation of a new chemistry.

Further, Lavoisier would utilize another subtle fluid from contemporary science, which he termed *caloric*, to explain the liberation of heat during the combustion process. Caloric was quite essential to his explanation of combustion and in a sense represented the displacement of one imponderable substance, phlogiston, by another, caloric. His use of caloric, however, was sufficiently different that it must not be construed as a substitute for phlogiston.[33]

Lavoisier's concept of a gas was that of a solid made aeriform by absorption of large amount of caloric. Thus, the gas oxygen was looked upon as a "basis of oxygen" combined with caloric. During combustion of charcoal the "basis of oxygen" combined with carbon to form carbonic acid (CO_2) while the caloric associated with the "basis of oxygen" was liberated as measurable heat. During calcination of lead, the "basis of oxygen" combined with lead to form lead oxide, while the caloric was liberated as sensible heat. The caloric theory came under attack even before the nineteenth century, when Count Rumford carried out his cannon-boring studies and caloric faded out of the picture by mid-nineteenth century when the energy concept was fully developed.

Another facet of Lavoisier's chemistry involved the role of oxygen as the acidifying principle.[34] He recognized very early that the combustion of carbon, sulfur, and phosphorus led to the formation of oxides having acidic characteristics when dissolved in water. He would argue that combination with the "basis of oxygen" resulted in the formation of acids. This position was carried to the point where he would look upon chlorine, not as an element but as the oxide of an undiscovered "muriaticum radical." Organic acids, such as acetic and oxalic, were looked upon as an organic radical combined with oxygen. This view of oxygen as literally, a "generator of acids" would cause problems even in his own day when Berthollet would point out that such mild acids as prussic acid (HCN) and sulfuretted hydrogen (H_2S) apparently contained no oxygen.[35] Furthermore, many metallic oxides were completely without acidic properties and, in fact, served as neutralizing agents toward acids. The theory of oxygen as an acidifying principle was totally demolished by Davy's work on chlorine in 1810.[36]

Of most lasting importance in Lavoisier's new chemistry, in addition to the conservation law, was the operational definition of simple bodies, or *elements*.[37] In setting forth his list of such substances in the *Traité* he was admittedly being speculative; some of his simple bodies might sometime be decomposed further, a point which he conceded. But his list of thirty-three elements would survive the ravages of time very well. Twenty-three of his simple bodies are recognized elements today. His three radicals all yielded genuine elements, as did his five "earths." Only *lumiére* and *calorique* fell into total discard. Even more important, the operational criterion for considering a substance elemental would prove of immense value as new candidates for the list were encountered during the next century.

The nomenclature book was an important adjunct to the new chemistry since it introduced a reform based on chemical composition. The new names had the advantage of consistency within the system and could lead to the abandonment of a multiplicity of names for the same substance. Moreoever, the nomenclature proposals had the subtle effect of favoring acceptance of the new chemistry if adopted.

The new chemistry unfolded gradually and reached a reasonable state of completeness only after 1789, although it can be argued that it would still require the incorporation of a chemical atomic theory, a fragment that would be added by Dalton early in the next century.[38] Thus, in retrospect Priestley was faced with a nebulous set of concepts for attack—concepts that continued to undergo addition and revision between 1780 and 1790.

Much of Lavoisier's new chemistry failed to survive the next quarter-century, even among enthusiastic followers. Oxygen as an acidifying principle fell by the wayside when Davy concluded that chlorine did not contain oxygen. Caloric as heat substance would vie for attention with the mechanical theory of heat and would totally succumb to the latter by 1850.

Even oxygen as the necessary ingredient in combustion and calcination came under suspicion in 1794 when the Dutch chemists revealed that combustion of metals could take place in hot sulfur[39] and succumbed further when Davy and others carried

	Noms nouveaux.	Noms anciens correfpondans.
	Lumière	Lumière.
Subftances fimples qui appartiennent aux trois règnes, (7 qu'on peut regarder comme les élémens des corps.	Calorique........	Chaleur. Principe de la chaleur. Fluide igné. Feu. Matière du feu & de la chaleur.
	Oxygène	Air déphlogiftiqué. Air empiréal. Air vital. Bafe de l'air vital.
	Azote..........	Gaz phlogiftiqué. Mofète. Bafe de la mofète.
	Hydrogène.......	Gaz inflammable. Bafe du gaz inflammable.
Subftances fimples non métalliques oxidables (7 acidifiables.	Soufre..........	Soufre.
	Phofphore	Phofphore.
	Carbone	Charbon pur.
	Radical muriatique .	Inconnu.
	Radical fluorique...	Inconnu.
	Radical boracique. .	Incoinu.
Subftances fimples métalliques oxidables (7 acidifiables.	Antimoine	Antimoine.
	Argent	Argent.
	Arfenic.........	Arfenic.
	Bifmuth	Bifmuth.
	Cobalt	Cobalt.
	Cuivre..........	Cuivre.
	Etain	Etain.
	Fer.............	Fer.
	Manganèfe.......	Manganèfe.
	Mercure	Mercure.
	Molybdène	Molybdène.
	Nickel..........	Nickel.
	Or.............	Or.
	Platine	Platine.
	Plomb	Plomb.
	Tungftène.......	Tungftène.
	Zinc	Zinc.
Subftances fimples falifiables terreufes.	Chaux..........	Terre calcaire, chaux.
	Magnéfie	Magnéfie, bafe du fel d'epfom.
	Baryte	Barote, terre pefante.
	Alumine	Argile, terre de l'alun, bafe de l'alun.
	Silice	Terre filiceufe, terre vitrifiable.

Lavoisier's Table of Elements. From Lavoisier, *Traité élémentaire de chimie,* 1789.

out combustions in chlorine. Such observations negated the importance of oxygen as an oxidizing agent.

Even those parts of the new chemistry that ultimately survived placed severe demands on those chemists who were believers. Lavoisier's operational definition of elements led to the discovery of a multiplicity of substances that apparently qualified, causing Davy to question whether there could be so many elements and causing him to give reconsideration in 1808 to a hypothesis that might integrate oxygen and plogiston into a harmonious system.[40]

The nomenclature proposals failed to attract converts among those who were unconvinced or lacked complete understanding of the new system. De la Metherie considered it not only in conflict with well-established terminology, but barbaric and misleading as well. Joseph Black, a professed adherent of Lavoisier's views on combustion, was openly antagonistic to the nomenclature.[41] Even the assumption that calcination produced oxides while reduction produced carbonic acid caused problems and became one of the focal points in Priestley's attack.

There is evidence that Priestley felt sympathy with some of the new views in the mid-eighties, but James Watt dissuaded Priestley from adopting Lavoisier's views.[42] The point arose after Lavoisier had decomposed water with hot iron, obtaining calx of iron and hydrogen in the process. Lavoisier considered the reaction supportive of his view that the hydrogen produced during the reaction of a metal with an acid came from the water. He had hypothesized that the metal first reacted with the water to form calx and hydrogen. Then the calx reacted with the acid (a nonmetallic oxide) to form salt.

$$\text{Metal} + \text{water} \longrightarrow \text{calx} + \text{hydrogen}$$
$$\text{Calx} + \text{acid} \longrightarrow \text{salt}$$

Or overall,

$$\text{Metal} + \text{water} + \text{acid} \longrightarrow \text{salt} + \text{hydrogen}$$

In his decomposition of steam by hot iron in 1883, Lavoisier felt that the evidence supported the first step in the metal-acid reaction. After Priestley had repeated Lavoisier's decomposition of steam by hot iron in 1785 he reported in a later work:

> I was for a long time of the opinion that his conclusion was just, and that the inflammable air was really furnished by the water being decomposed in the process; but though I continued to be of this opinion for some time, the frequent repetition of the experiments, with the light which Mr. Watt's observations threw upon them, satisfied me at length that the inflammable air came from the charcoal or the iron.[43]

Relevant to the above quote, Watt had been a participant in an unpleasant controversy regarding the nature of water, which involved a number of other scientists including Cavendish and Lavoisier. Sometime before 1781 Priestley as well as others had observed that when inflammable and either common or dephlogisticated airs are burned, dew is observed in the apparatus.[44] Watt developed a rational explanation based on the supposition that dephlogisticated air was water lacking in phlogiston but containing matter of heat while inflammable air was phlogiston. During the reaction a redistribution of phlogiston and loss of heat led to production of normal water.[45]

In the meantime, Cavendish not only confirmed Priestley's observations but went on to prepare a significant quantity of the "dew" and ultimately establish that it had the qualities of pure water.[46] Observations similar to those of Priestley had also been made in France by Macquer, de la Metherie, and Lavoisier and associates. In June 1783 Lavoisier and Laplace burned hydrogen and oxygen in an appropriate apparatus in the presence of several academicians and Charles Blagden of the Royal Society. Blagden had discussed Cavendish's work at the time and later implied that Lavoisier sought credit for discoveries that more properly belonged to Cavendish. Watt was also involved since he believed that he had established that water is the product of the reaction before either Cavendish or Lavoisier. There is little question that it was Cavendish who first established that pure water is the product of combustion of inflammable air and dephlogisticated air. However, his understanding of the reaction, like that of Watt, was overlaid with phlogistic explanations.[47] Lavoisier saw clearly, on the basis of experiments involving both synthesis and decomposition, that water might be looked upon as a compouond of hydrogen and oxygen.[48] This view became another important component of the new chemistry.

In the light of the above, Priestley momentarily wavered toward Lavoisier's position, at least on certain specific points, but was brought back to the phlogiston position by Watt. From that point forward Priestley's position against the new chemistry became steadily more firm, but it was particularly after reaching America that his pen flowed freely in opposition to the anti-phlogistic views.[49] Richard Kirwan carried on the principal campaign in defense of phlogiston late in the eighties,[50] but the care with which Kirwan's arguments were answered by Lavoisier and his associates made Kirwan a convert in 1791.[51]

It must not be assumed, however, that Priestley was unique among first rank chemists in his objection to the Lavoisier views. Schofield commented on this point very clearly a decade ago:

> Seen in this framework, one is forced to inquire not why Priestley failed to accept the theory of oxidation, but rather why he should have been singled out, for so much attention, from the class of all those men who did not accept it.[52]

Schofield then calls attention to other prominent chemists who were unconverted to the new chemistry, men who included Scheele, Bergman, Cavendish, Macquer, and Richter. Even in the next century Davy would seek to reconcile the phlogiston and oxygen views.

During the years when his peers of earlier days were dying or being silenced, Priestley fought on against the theory of oxidation until his transigence became the same kind of unorthodoxy found in his political and theological views. Priestley was not a man to adopt an opinion because it was held by the majority; neither was his opposition that of unreasoning and unreasonable reaction. It is necessary to examine the methods by which the new chemistry was propagated, the arguments used to support it, and the circumstances in which Priestley met them, before his continued support of Phlogiston can be seen as more than the blind conservatism of an old man.[53]

Priestley found plenty of issues on which to focus his attack. One of the most interesting is the case of "finery cinder," the black oxide of iron. Priestley pointed out that when "finery cinder" undergoes reduction with charcoal, the products are iron and inflammable air. However, according to Lavoisier's chemistry the products should have been iron and fixed air.[54]

Priestley's criticism was a valid one within the chemistry of the day but is confused by the failure of chemists to distinguish clearly between several flammable gases and particularly by his own doggedness in looking upon all such gases as being essentially alike in being loaded with phlogiston.[55] As Cruikshank soon pointed out, the inflammable air was not hydrogen but a lower oxide of carbon (carbon monoxide).[56] Despite Cruikshank's objection, Priestley continued his criticism on the basis of his concept of the nature of inflammable airs and on the grounds that according to the new chemistry fixed air would have been expected.[57]

In the light of the unsatisfactory nature of many facets of the new chemistry, coupled with a mass of experimental facts open to a variety of theoretical interpretations, it is not an obvious conclusion that Priestley was blindly stubborn in refusing to become a convert to the new chemistry. In the course of his objections he was raising questions that were causing adherents of the new views to sharpen their explanations.

PERSONALITY CONFLICTS

In retrospect it is hard to avoid brief speculation on whether personality conflicts may have been involved in the relationships between Lavoisier and Priestley. Was their failure to agree on the same chemistry an inevitable part of the human desire for recognition, a desire from which scientists are not immune?[58]

Lavoisier was a proud and ambitious man. His perceptive and logical mind caused him to recognize a new and fruitful way to organize chemical facts, even when his perceptive conclusions were not solidly supported by sound experimental evidence. Yet there is a hint of arrogance in Lavoisier's behavior. While he was frequently gracious to distant predecessors in his evaluation of the science that led up to his experiments, he was frequently thoughtless toward those contemporaries whose work contributed toward the development of his ideas.

In his writings he could ignore completely the prior contributions of Bayen, Cadet, Scheele, and Priestley. He would misspell Priestley's name and allocate to himself equal credit alongside Scheele and Priestley in the discovery of oxygen. He would delete reference to the nitrous air test in the final version of his ''Easter Memoir,'' rather than acknowledge that Priestley's criticism had steered him in the right direction. His behavior in the water controversy led to a situation where the ruffled feelings of Watt and Cavendish would remain forever unhealed. Even his close associates, Guyton de Morveau and Fourcroy, failed to rise to his defense during his troubles with the revolutionary government.

Carelessness and distortion on Lavoisier's part in recognition of the work of others may well have been a source of irritation to Priestley, humble and forgiving on the surface, but nevertheless sensitive and proud. It is obviously speculative to suggest that personal antagonisms may have been a factor in the failure of Priestley and Lavoisier to collaborate harmoniously, but the suspicion is difficult to negate. Both were proud and both were eager for priority.

However, the principal factor in Priestley's failure to accept the new chemistry lies in the shortcomings of the new chemistry itself. In the context of the times, a good experimentalist familiar with the detailed facts of chemistry would find valid objections to the explanations provided by the new chemistry. With his own views of the nature of matter and his success in chemical experimentation on a qualitative basis there was no compelling reason for him to adopt the new point of view, however compelling such facts as weight gain of the metal on calcination might be. The failure of Priestley to switch is understandable within the context of his times. It is only when viewed from a much later vantage point, with eyes blinded to the limitations of knowledge at the end of the eighteenth century, that Priestley's position appears anomalous.

NOTES

1. J. Priestley, *Experiments and Observations on Different Kinds of Air*, 3 vols. (London, 1774, 1775, 1777), 2: 36-38. Priestley's work on gases was published primarily in these three volumes and in three later volumes entitled *Experiments and Observations Relating to Various Branches of Philosophy; with a Continuation of the Observations of Air* (London, 1779), 1781, 1786). Hereafter these six volumes will be cited as *E and O* with volume number and pages. References are to the first edition unless otherwise indicated.
2. P. Bayen, Expériences faites sur le précipité de la dissolution mercuriella l'acide nitreux par l'alkali fixe, *Observations sur la Physique* 3, (1774): 134-35. This journal is referred to as "Rozier's journal" in the text.
3. P. Bayen, Recherches sur la cause de l'augmentation de poids qu'eprouve le mercure l'alkali fixe, *ibid.*, pp. 284-92.
4. Antoine Lavoisier, *Oeuvres de Lavoisier*, ed. J.B.A. Dumas, 6 vols. (Paris, 1862-93), 4: 190.
5. U. Boklund, A lost letter from Scheele to Lavoisier, *Lychnos* 17 (1957-58): 39-62.
6. E. Grimaux, Une lettre inédite de Scheele a Lavoisier, *Revue Générales des Science pure et appliquées* 1 (1890): 2. Also see ibid., pp. 49, 55 and passim.
7. S. J. French, The Chemical Revolution—The Second Phase, *Journal of Chemical Education*, 27 (1950): 83-89; D. I. Duveen and H. S. Klickstein, *A Bibliography of the Works of Antoine Laurent Lavoisier, 1743-1794*, (London, 1954), pp. 34-38.
8. *E and O*, 2: 40.

9. J. Priestley, On nitrous air, *Philosophical Transactions of the Royal Society,* 62 (1771): 210.

10. *E and O,* 1: 110-11.

11. Ibid., 2: 40.

12. Ibid., p. 46.

13. Ibid., pp. 48-49.

14. J. Priestley, An Account of further discoveries in air, *Philosophical Transactions of the Royal Society,* 65 (1775): 384.

15. A. L. Lavoisier, Mémoire sur la nature du principe qui se combine avec les Metaux pendant leur calcination, & qui en augmente le poids, *Observations sur la physique,* 5 (1775): 429-33.

16. Ibid., p. 433.

17. *E and O,* 2: 320.

18. M. Berthelot, *La révolution chimique Lavoisier,* (Paris, 1890), pp. 254, 264-65, 270-71.

19. A. L. Lavoisier, *Traité élémentaire de chimie,* 2 vols. (Paris, 1789), 1: 42-47; or see A. L. Lavoisier, *Elements of Chemistry,* Trans. R. Kerr. (Edinburgh, 1790), pp. 33-37; or A. J. Ihde, *The Development of Modern Chemistry,* (New York, 1964), pp. 65-67.

20. A. L. Lavoisier, Memoire sur la calcination de l'Etain dans les vaisseaux fermés; et sur la cause de l'augmentation de poids qu'acquièrent ce Métal pendant cette opoeration, *Mémoirs de l'Académie Royale des Sciences,* (1774), p. 351 (publ. in 1778). The original version of this paper was submitted on 14 April 1774, read on 12 November 1774 and published under the title Mémoir sur la calcination des Métaux dans les vaisseaux fermés, & sur la cause de l'augmentation de poids qu'ils acquièrent pendant cette operation in *Observations sur la physique,* 4 (1774): 446. The revised version was submitted to the Académie on 10 May 1777. Both versions deal with calcination of metals but notable changes were made in the final version.

21. A. L. Lavoisier, Considérations Générales sur la Nature des Acides, Et sur les Principes dont ils sont composés, *Mémoires de l'Academie Royale des Sciences,* (1778), p. 535 (publ. in 1781).

22. A. L. Lavoisier, Mémoire sur la nature du Principe qui se combine avec les Métaux pendant leur calcination, & qui en augmente le poids, *Mémoires de l'Académie Royale des Sciences,* (1775), pp. 520-26 (publ. in 1778). For original version see n. 15.

23. A. L. Lavoisier, *Mémoires de Chimie,* collected by Mme. M. A. Lavoisier, 2 vols. (Paris, 1805), 2: 1-17. This is not a reprint of the "Easter Memoir" but a rewritten paper based on it and related experiments.

24. A. L. Lavoisier, *Oeuvres de Lavoisier,* ed. Dumas, 2: 122-28.

25. J.B. Conant, *The Overthrow of the Phlogiston Theory,* (Cambridge, 1950), p. 22-28.

26. Duveen and Klickstein, *A Bibliography. . . ,* pp. 33-73. See n. 7.

27. L B. Guyton de Morveau, A. L. Lavoisier, C. L. Berthollet and A. F. de Fourcroy, *Méthode de nomenclature chimique,* (Paris, 1787).

28. See n. 19.

29. Duveen and Klickstein, *A Bibliography...*, pp. 68-93. Of particular importance is the paper entitled "Reflections sur le Phlogistique, Pour servir de développement à la theorie de la Combustion & de la Calcination, publiée en 1777, *Mémoires de l'Académie Royale des Sciences,* (1783), pp. 505-38 (publ. 1786). This paper is treated by Lavoisier as a sequel to his 1777 paper, "Mémoir sur la Combustion en Général," *Mémoires de l'Académie Royale des Sciences,* (1777), 592-600 (publ. in 1780). In 1774 an anonymous attack on phlogiston, "Discours sur le Phlogistique et sur plusieurs points importans in Chymie," *Observations sur la Physique,* 3 (1774), 183-98 is usually attributed to Lavoisier.

30. Lavoisier, *Traité élémentaire de chimie,* Kerr Trans. pp. 130-31.

31. S. Hales, *Vegetable Staticks,* (London, 1827), pp. 95-105.

32. J. Parascandola and A. J. Ihde, History of the Pneumatic Trough, *Isis,* 60, (1969): 351-61.

33. Lavoisier, *Traité élémentaire de chimie,* pp. 1-25, 54-65. Also see, R. Morris, Lavoisier and the caloric theory, *British Journal of the History of Science,* 6 (1972): 1-38.

34. Ibid., pp. 54-77.

35. C. L. Berthollet, Sur l'acide prussique, *Mémoires de l'Académie Royale des Sciences,* (1787), pp. 148-62 (publ. 1789); Extrait d'une memoire sur l'acide Prussique, *Annales de Chimie,* 1, (1789): 30-39; Suite des expériences sur l'acide sulfureux, ibid., 2 (1789): 54-72, p. 68; A. F. de Fourcroy, Mémoire sur l'esprit recteur de Boerrhaave, l'arome des chimiste francais, ou le principe de l'odeur des végétaux, *ibid.,* 25 (1798): 233.

36. H. Davy, Researches on the oxymuriatic acid, its nature and combinations, and on the elements of the muriatic acid with some experiments on sulfur and phosphorus, *Philosophical Transactions of the Royal Society,* 100 (1810): 231-57; or Alembic Club Reprint, no. 9, *The Elementary Nature of Chlorine,* (Edinburgh, 1953). Also see R. Siegfried, Humphry Davy and the Elementary Nature of Chlorine, *Journal of Chemical Education,* 36 (1959): 568-70.

37. Lavoisier, *Traité élémentaire de chimie,* Kerr Trans. pp. 175-76.

38. J. Dalton, *A New System of Chemical Philosophy* (Manchester, vol. 1, pt. 1, 1908; pt. 2, 1810; vol. 2, 1827).

39. J. R. Deiman, A. Paets van Troostwijk, P. Nieuwland, N. Bondt, and A. Lâuwerenburg, "Expériences sur l'inflammation du mélange du saufre et des métaux sans la présence de l'oxygène." *Rescherches Physico-chimiques,* 3 (1794): 71-96.

40. H. Davy, New researches on the nature of certain bodies, being an appendix to the Bakerian Lecture of 1808, *Philosophical Transactions of the Royal Society,* 99 (1809): 450-70; also see R. Siegfried, An Attempt in the United States to resolve the differences between the oxygen and the phlogiston theories, *Isis,* 46 (1955): 327-36 and Humphry Davy and the elementary nature of chlorine, *Journal of Chemical Education,* 36 (1959): 568-70.

41. J. C. de la Metherie, Méthode de nomenclature chimique, *Observations sur la physique,* 31 (1787): 210-19; Essai sur la nomenclature chimique, ibid., pp. 270-85; Discours preliminaire, ibid., 32 (1788): 12; Defense de l'hygrométre a cheveu; chapt. vii: De la retrogration, ibid., p. 35; Objets de Recherches, extraits d'un manuscrit sur les ventes, ibid., pp. 75-76; J. Black, *Lectures on the Elements of Chemistry,* ed. J. Robison (Edinburgh, 1803); 1 492-93, 555. Also see M. P. Crosland, *Historical Studies in the Language of Chemistry,* (Cambridge, 1962), pp. 193-214.

42. P. G. Hartog, Joseph Priestley and his place in the History of Science, *Proceedings of the Royal Institution,* 26 (1931): 395-430; The newer views of Priestley and Lavoisier, *Annals of Science,* 5 (1941): 1-56.

43. J. Priestley, *E and O,* 1790 ed., 1: 276.

44. J. Priestley, *E and O,* 5 (1881); Dr. Priestley's experiments relating to phlogiston and the seeming conversion of water into air, *Philosophical Transactions of the Royal Society,* 73 (1783): 426.

45. J. Watt, Thoughts on the constituent parts of water and of dephlogisticated air; with an account on some experiments on that subject, *Philosophical Transactions of the Royal Society,* 74 (1784): 329; Sequel to thoughts on the constituent parts of water, ibid., p. 354.

46. H. Cavendish, Experiments on air, *Philosophical Transactions of the Royal Society,* 74 (1784): 119-53; or see Alembic Club Reprint, No. 3, *Experiments on Air* (Edinburgh, 1950).

47. For a brief account of the controversy see A. J. Ihde, *The Development of Modern Chemistry,* (New York, 1964), pp. 69-73; for greater detail with reference to all relevant literature see J. R. Partington, *A History of Chemistry,* (London, 1962), 3, 325-38, 344-62, 436-56.

48. J. B. M. C. Meusnier and A. L. Lavoisier, Mémoire Où l'on prouve par la décomposition de l'Eau, qui ce Fluide n'est point une substance simple, & qu'il y a plusieurs moyens d'obtenir en grand l'Air inflammable qui y entre comme principe constituant, *Mémoires de l'Académie Royale des Sciences,* (1781): 269-83 (publ. 1784); Lavoisier, Mémoire Dans lequel on a pour object de prouver que l'Eau n'est une substance simple, un élément proprement dit, mais qu'elle est susceptible du décomposition & de recomposition, ibid., 468-493.

49. Partington, *A History of Chemistry,* 2, pp. 293-95, has a complete listing of Priestley's papers written in America and published in Nicholson's *Journal of Natural Philosophy, Chemistry, and the Arts* (five papers), *Transactions of the American Philosophical Society* (ten papers), and S. L. Mitchill's *Medical Repository* (twenty-six papers). In this period he also published several books which dealth with the phlogiston problem (see Partington, *A History of Chemistry,* 2, pp. 244-45), the most important being *The Doctrine of Phlogiston Established and that of the Composition of Water Refuted* (Northumberland, Pa., 1800); 2d ed. with additions, 1803.

50. R. Kirwan, *An Essay on Phlogiston and the Constitution of Acids,* (London, 1784).

51. R. Kirwan, *Essai sur le Phlogistique, et sur la Constitution des Acides,* traduit, avec des notes de MM. de Morveau, Lavoisier, de la Place, Monge, Berthollet, et de Fourcroy, (Paris, 1788). This edition is a translation by Mme. Lavoisier with extensive refutations by the French chemists listed. Kirwan reissued the book in English with translation of the notes by the French chemists by Wm. Nicholson and "Remarks upon the annotations" by Kirwan (London, 1789). Also see the Kirwan letter to L. Crell, publ. in *Chemische Annalen für die Freunde der Naturlehre,* 1 (1791): 425.

52. R. E. Schofield, Joseph Priestley, the nature of oxidation and the nature of matter, *Journal of the History of Ideas,* 25 (1964): 285-94, p. 286.

53. Ibid., p. 287.

54. J. Priestley, A Reply to Mr. Cruickshank's Observations in Defense of the new system of chemistry, *Medical Repositor,* 5 (1802): 390.

55. J. Priestley, *E and O,* 1 (1774): 55, 65, 68; *E and O,* 6 (1786): 11, 406.

56. W. Cruickshank, Observations and Experiments relating to the Pile of Volta, *Journal of Natural Philosophy, Chemistry, and the Arts,* new series, 1 (1801): 201; Observations in answer to Dr. Priestley's memoir in Defense of the Doctrine of Phlogiston, ibid., 2 (1802): 42.

57. J. Priestley, A reply to Mr. Cruickshank's observations in defense of the new system of chemistry, in the Philosophical Journal, ibid., 1 (1801): 181, on the air from finery cinder and charcoal, with other remarks on the experiments and observations of Mr. Cruickshank, ibid., 3 (1802): 52, Answer to the observations of Mr. Cruickshank upon the Doctrine of Phlogiston, *ibid.,* 4 (1803): 65.

58. See, for example, J. D. Watson, *The Double Helix* (New York, 1968); F. E. Manuel, *A Portrait of Isaac Newton,* Cambridge, Mass., 1968).

3

Joseph Priestley and the Physicalist Tradition in British Chemistry

ROBERT E. SCHOFIELD

Iowa State University

When Joseph Priestley wrote to Theophilus Lindsey in February 1770, "I am now taking up some of Dr. Hale's inquiries concerning air," he was not only defining his area of future study but also, as it turned out, the mode of its investigation.[1] The "inquiries concerning air" were those of the Rev. Dr. Stephen Hales. They were embodied in a long chapter (ninety-two pages and over forty percent of the whole) of a book on plant physiology, *Vegetable Staticks,* first published in 1727.[2] For all its demonstrable influence on the chemists of mid-eighteenth century, this is a chapter curiously lacking in chemical tone. Its inspiration is derived from botany, its methodology from hydrodynamics, and its ontology from the physics of Isaac Newton.[3] Yet, these same characteristics are to be found in Priestley's work on gases—in its repeated concern with living processes, its constant use of volume and pressure changes as experimental metrics, and its increasing reiteration of Newtonian physical arguments and analogies as explanatory hypotheses. Priestley's chemical researches, it has been said, were marked by an unex-

92

pected conservatism, but that conservatism lay not so much in his persistent defense of phlogiston or of elementary water but rather in his adoption of a scientific worldview nearly forty years out-of-date when he commenced his ''chemical'' studies. Indeed, it will be argued in this essay that Priestley's work is most clearly to be distinguished from that of most of his contemporaries, in its successes as well as its failures, by his continuation of a physicalist tradition of chemistry, derived immediately from the work of Stephen Hales, indirectly from that of John Freind and of Newton himself, and ultimately from a pattern set by the so-called Father of British Chemistry, Robert Boyle.

Now Boyle is most often identified as the ''skeptical Chymist,'' who argued vigorously against scholastic and Paracelsian chemical theories. It is less frequently noted that he was not at all skeptical about the nature of the theory that ought to replace these two. From the titles of his more typical works, usually involving some version of ''mechanical origin of forms and qualities,'' as well as from the content of nearly everything he wrote on scientific subjects, it is clear that Robert Boyle had adopted the essential features of the mechanical philosophy of the seventeenth century.[4] He was too canny, one might almost say too British, to involve himself deeply in the arcane metaphysical arguments that divided Cartesian corpuscularians from Gassendian atomists; but whatever their position on the existence of the void, the ultimate divisibility of matter, or the relation of mind to body, the mechanical philosophers agreed in their attempts to reduce all physical phenomena to problems of kinematics. With an admirable singleness of purpose, Boyle set himself the task of demonstrating that chemical phenomena also were explicable in terms of the size, shape, and motion of the material particles of which the world was made.

Boyle wrote in *The Excellency and Grounds of the Corpuscular or Mechanical Philosophy* of 1674, that:

if the chymists, or others that would deduce a complete natural philosophy from salt, sulphur, and mercury, or any other set number of ingredients of things, would well consider, what they undertake, they might easily discover, that the material parts of bodies, as such, can reach but to a small part of the phaenomena of nature, whilst these ingredients are considered but as quiescent things, and therefore they would find themselves necessitated to suppose them to be active, and that things purely corpeal cannot be but by means of local motion, and the effects, that may result from that, accompanying variqusly shaped, sized and aggregated parts of matter.[5]

Convinced though he was of the general validity of the mechanical philosophy, Boyles was never prepared to insist upon his own particular applications of it. His accounts were, he declared, merely demonstrations of the possibility of explicating forms and qualities mechanically.[6] Examination of those accounts will show the wisdom of such restraint. Without an independent means of determining the various mechanical parameters, sizes, shapes, and motions of particles could be, and were, multiplied by Boyle and his immediate successors until they rivaled in number the forms and qualities they were expected to replace.

An example of this problem is to be found in application of Boyle's explanation of the nature of corrosive menstrua, from the *Mechanical Origin and Production of Qualities* of 1675. These consist, he says, of corpuscles that are small enough to get into the pores of the body to be dissolved, yet not so small as to pass through them, not so slender or flexible as to be unable to disjoin the parts they invade, "agile and advantaged for motion." "Whereby the engaged corpuscles, like so many little wedges and levers, may be enabled to wrench open, or force asunder the little parts between which they have insinuated themselves."[7] In 1690, the Cartesian disciple of Boyle, Nicolas Lemery, set himself to adapt this view, for his popular *Cours de Chymie*, to an explanation of why *aqua regia* will dissolve gold but not silver, while *aqua fortis* dissolves silver, but not gold. In *aqua regia,* Lemery argues, the points of nitric acid particles are so blunted by spirit of salt as to be unable to penetrate the pores of silver, though they can penetrate the larger pores of the more malleable gold, dislodging its particles. In *aqua fortis*, the fine points of unblunted nitric acid particles penetrate the pores of silver, disjoining its particles, but they pass through the pores of gold.[8]

Now this *is* an ingenious mechanical explanation, but so also is that of Guillaume Hombeg, also a disciple of Boyle, who argues, in 1706, that in *aqua fortis*, the points of nitric acid are too large to penetrate the finer pores of dense gold, while they penetrate and disjoin silver. In combination, as *aqua regia,* the slender particles of spirit of salt are strengthened and impelled by particles of nitric acid as they disjoin gold, but pass through the pores of silver.[9]

Clearly a kinematic, mechanistic chemistry, unable to discriminate finally between diametrically opposed explanations such as these, was too inconclusive ultimately to survive. On the Continent chemists either turned away from mechanistic chemistry entirely and, with Becher and Stahl, developed a substance-focused experimentalism that was to flower in Lavoisier's elemental chemistry, or they retained a mechanistic faith in theory, but, like Lemery himself or Herman Boerhaave, in practical application adopted empirical attitudes. In Britain the immediate reaction was different. There, Isaac Newton provided an alternative to kinematic physicalist chemistry in his development of a dynamical corpuscularity through the addition of interparticulate central forces to the parameters of size, shape, and motion.

This adding of force to make dynamics out of kinematics was anything but easy, conceptually or polemically. Although the *Principia* of 1687 had demonstrated the inadequacy of purely kinematic considerations in the explanation of phenomena, its philosophical justification of the concept of force was ambivalent to the point of equivocation and his opponents accused Newton of reintroducing occult qualities into science. Nonetheless, he succeeded in proving the quantitative efficacy of long-range attractive forces in explicating some phenomena and showed that repulsive forces, acting inversely as the distance between adjacent gas particles, permits the derivation of Boyle's law. He declares, in the Preface to the *Principia,* that having demonstrated the mathematical deduction of long-ranged forces from celestial phenomena and then deduced the motions of the planets from these forces:

> I wish we could derive the rest of the phenomena of Nature by the same kind of reasoning from mechanical principles, for I am induced by many reasons to suspect that they may all depend upon certain forces by which the particles of bodies, by some causes hitherto unknown, are either mutually impelled towards one another and cohere in regular figures, or are repelled and recede from one another.[10]

Illustration of the potency of force arguments for some of these other phenomena of nature follows in Newton's *Opticks* of 1704, and especially in its Latin edition of 1706, where the added queries take up consideration of the fundamental nature of matter—and therefore touch on chemical considerations.

> . . .it seems probable to me,'' Newton writes in Query 23, ''that God in the Beginning form'd Matter in solid, massy, hard impenetrable, moveable Particles, of such Sizes and Figures, and with such other Properties, and in such Proportion to Space, as most conduced to the End for which he formed them. . .And. . .that Nature may be lasting, the Changes of corporeal Things are to be placed only in the various Separations and new Associations and Motions of these permanent Particles. . .[11]

Now these separations and new associations are to take place as a consequence of active principles, or forces, and Newton explicitly names such phenomena as deliquescence, chemical composition, double decomposition, ebullition, dissolution, concretion, crystallization, and congelation as examples of attractive forces in action. Then ''as in Algebra, where affirmative Quantities vanish and cease, there negative ones begin; so in Mechanicks, where

Attraction ceases, there a repulsive Virtue ought to succeed''— and Newton follows with examples of phenomena produceable by repulsive forces, including volatility and evaporation, fermentation and putrefaction, elasticity and disjunction. And finally, he declares:

> To derive two or three general Principles of Motion from Phaenomena, and afterwards to tell us how the Properties and Actions of all corporeal Things follow from these manifest Principles, would be a very great step in Philosophy, though the causes of those Principles were not yet discover'd.[12]

Little wonder, with such encouragement from the two canonical works of eighteenth-century natural philosophy, that British successors to Newton ignored the pseudoagnosticism of his attitude toward the real existence of forces and set themselves to realizing the Newtonian imperative: from the motions, find the forces, from the forces, deduce the phenomena. Subsequent editions of the *Principia* (for instance, the second edition of 1713) and the second English edition of the *Opticks* (1717) were to add scholia or queries that were ultimately to dilute the authority of this early dynamic corpuscularity, but well before these second thoughts of Newton had appeared, a school of Newtonians had been writing, commenting on, and expanding Newton's dynamicist ideas. The most important of these, from the view of physicalist chemistry, were John Keill, John Freind, and Roger Cotes.

Keill was one of the earliest supporters of Newtonian natural philosophy, and his text of 1702, *Introductio ad veram Physicam*, was the first independent schoolbook on the subject. In 1708 Keill wrote a paper for the *Philosophical Transactions of the Royal Society*, ''On the Laws of Attraction and other Physical Properties,'' which repeats material from the chemical Query 23 of the recently published Latin *Opticks*, and attempts to show, in rather more specific detail than Newton, how attractive forces, decreasing in some greater ratio than the square of distance, when added to the size and shape and motion of primitive, homogeneous particles, might explain the chemical phenomena cited in that query.[13]

One of his suggestions, involving different attractions between particles of a body and between these and those of a menstruum as an approach to explanation of dissolution, was taken up and further expanded by John Freind, whose *Praelectiones Chymiae* was published in 1709.[14] Freind presented a thoroughgoing physicalist approach to chemistry in his lectures. He concerned himself only with the mechanisms of chemical operations and ignored any concern for the persistent nature of elementary substances. Indeed, Freind tended to the notion that there were no such permanent classifications, for all that mattered were the ultimate homogeneous particles and the attractive forces between them. Like Keill, Freind uses particle size and shape, motion, momentum, and different forces of attraction as his operative variables, and, like Keill, he is necessarily restricted to qualitative argument. A typical explanation is *his* approach to that vexing question relating to gold and silver, *aqua regia* and *aqua fortis:*

> If the attraction of gold be to that of silver, as *a* to *b*, of silver to *aqua fortis* as *b* to *d,* and of *aqua fortis* to *aqua regia* as *d* to *e,* and if *f* be the magnitude of *aqua fortis* particles, *r* be that of *aqua regia* particles, *c* the cohesion of gold, and *g* that of silver; then should *f* be greater than the pores of gold, *aqua fortis* will never dissolve gold, however large be *d*. But if *b-d* x *f* exceed *g*, with *f* less than the pores of silver, than *aqua fortis* will dissolve silver, while if *b-e* x *r* is less than *g*, silver will not dissolve in *aqua regia*, whatever its pore size might be. And if *a-e* x *r* be greater than *c*, *aqua regia* will be able to dissolve gold.[15]

Two things, in particular, must be observed respecting Freind's physicalist chemistry in addition to the painfully obvious consideration that no values can be assigned to his ''quantities.'' It does not concern itself with air (gases) and, like Keill's work, avoids any consideration of repulsive forces. Why this latter should be so, in the face of Newton's explicit use of repulsion, is hard to say, but the majority of early Newtonians were clearly reluctant to ascribe both attractive and repulsive forces to the same fundamental particles. The involvement of air in chemical processes, at that time, was generally confined to its supposed operation as an instrument, but not a constituent, in chemical change. For the consideration of constituent air by Stephen Hales, the next significant figure in the British physicalist tradition, and particularly for Hales's use of repulsive forces—a major and distinguishing characteristic—one must find an influence other than that of John Freind, whose "ingenious *Rationale* of the chief operations in Chymistry" is the only chemical work, other than Newton's *Opticks,* explicitly cited by Hales.[16]

It seems clear that the other influence must have been that of Roger Cotes, whose lectures on hydrostatics and pneumatics Hales had heard while resident at Cambridge as a Fellow of Corpus Christi.[17] Cotes does concern himself with repulsive forces in adopting Newton's explanation for the elasticity of air. He also employs attractive forces, as John Keill had done before him, in explaining the capillary rise of sap in plants—a matter of concern to Hales. In the experimental demonstrations by Cotes and William Whiston, which accompanied the lectures on pneumatics, the mercury manometer, which Hales was later to adapt so fruitfully, had been demonstrated.[18] Finally, in a lecture entitled "Air sometimes generated, sometimes consumed; the nature of factitious airs, explosions in vacuo, dissolutions, fermentations, &c.," Cotes had discussed, but not explained, some phenomena similar to those which Hales was to address in his own chapter on air.[19]

It was in that chapter: "A Specimen of an attempt to analyze the Air by a great variety of chymio-statical Experiments, which shew in how great a proportion Air is wrought into the composition of animal, vegetable and mineral Substances, and withal how readily it resumes its former elastic state, when in the dissolution of those Substances it is disengaged from them," which marked the true beginning of pneumatic chemistry—though it was to develop in a way vastly different from that which Hales would have expected. He was led to his study of airs through the observation of the quantities rising spontaneously through the sap during his experiments on plant physiology. Yet he did not, in fact, analyze this *air*, as we should understand that term. Indeed, it seems never to have occured to Hales that there were different varieties of airs in those quantities which he "released" from substances in his experiments. What fascinated Hales about air, fascinated him to the point of near-obsession in his later years, was not the quality of its substance, but the nature of its activity. For Hales saw, as no previous person but Newton had seen, that *both* attraction and repulsion were together necessary in an active organized universe.

> "If all the parts of matter," Hales wrote, "were only endued with a strongly attracting power, whole nature would then immediately become one unactive cohering lump; wherefore it was absolutely necessary, in order to the actuating and enlivening this vast mass of attracting matter, that there should be everywhere intermixed with it a due proportion of strongly repelling elastick particles, which might enliven the whole mass, by the incessant action between them and the attracting particles.[20]

This was the role Hales saw for the air—as the strongly repelling elastic particles enlivening the mass.

In the course of his experiments, Hales was to discover, however, that air was more than an elastic repelling and enlivening substance. It was a "protean principle." Under normal conditions its particles repel one another, but are attracted by those of other matter (acids, sulphurs, salts, etc.) floating in it that reduce its elasticity; under some circumstances the particles of air might become fixed, bound, and unelastic in other bodies where they contribute to the union of concreted matter. By suitable processes of distillation (i.e., heating) or fermentation (i.e., mixing with acids, alkalies, water, etc.), these fixed-air particles might be roused out of their spheres of attraction and into those of repulsion, to become free elastic air again, enlivening and disjoining the solid substance in which they had been fixed.

These, then, were the types of experiments that Hales performed—in which various quantities of air, measured by volume and/or pressure, were released from or, alternately, were fixed in substances. During these processes Hales must, as we should interpret his experiments, have obtained a variety of different gases (carbon monoxide and dioxide, nitrous and nitric acid, sulphur dioxide, ammonia, hydrogen, and oxygen), but he never recognized qualitative differences in his airs. When he describes variations in their behavior—for instance, the inflammability of that released by the ''fermentation'' of iron in acid, he ascribes the anomaly to the presence of adventitious unelastic particles in the air.

These experiments were essentially to be the last in chemistry performed by Stephen Hales, and they mark also the end of a *continuous* physicalist tradition in British chemistry. One English chemist, John Mickleburgh, taught chemistry at Cambridge in the Freind-Hales mode until 1741, but his lectures were never published.[21] The general influence of Hales's reductionist ideas was felt by Jean Théophile Desaguliers and by John Rowning, but neither were chemists. The widespread chemical influence of Hales's work is to be seen in the chemical studies of Boerhaave, and then in the continental tradition, which merges with Stahlian chemistry, and in the experiments of the Scot Joseph Black. Boerhaave's famous lectures in chemistry were modified between their unofficial publication of 1724 and their official appearance as the *Elementa Chemiae* of 1732, to accomodate Hales's discovery of the constituent role of air in chemistry.[22] This substantial orientation of Hales's work was emphasized again by Macquer and by Rouelle, Lavoisier's teacher. More significantly, aspects of Hales's work were pursued by Black, who was so inspired by Hales's discovery of the amount of fixed air released by ''fermentation'' from *vesicle calculi,* that he initially adopted that subject for his M.D. thesis.[23] Black was surely also impressed by Hales's somewhat confusing observation that the causticity of calcined lime was, in some way, to be related to the sulphureous and elastic air particles so agitated by heat as to become "fire particles," that are fixed in lime and subsequently released in its dissolution.[24] However, before Black was to examine this observation and invert it in his discovery of a particular species of air, he had already received instruction in the nature of chemistry, which was very different from the physicalist approach characteristic of Hales.

Now Hales may also be given some of the credit—or blame—for this turn of events. In an appendix to his second book, the *Haemastatics* of 1733, he was to observe that it seemed impossible to pry into the various positions of the particles, in their several combinations to account on mechanical principles for the effects produced.[25] A year later the Dutch scientist Peter van Musschenbrock was also to write, in his *Elementa Physicae*, that since one cannot perform experiments on the fundamental particles nor determine how they combine, nor what the shapes, and so forth, of their combinations might be, one could not determine their various forces of attraction.[26] But if these, the fundamental parameters of physicalist chemistry, could not be determined, of what use were they in providing explanations of phenomena? Georg Ernst Stahl had been asking that question as early as the 1720s, and the introduction into Britain of Stahlian chemistry in translations by Peter Shaw and William Lewis was to make explicit an antimechanistic chemical theory.

In the notes of his 1727 translation of Boerhaave, Shaw had praised Newton, John Keill, and John Freind as having solved almost all the phenomena that chemistry presents. In his 1741 translation of Boerhaave, which follows upon a translation of Stahl's *Fundamenta Chymiae*, that praise was severely moderated by the observation that until its properties were ascertained, attraction was too fertile a principle to apply so precipitously.[27] By 1755 Shaw was declaring, in his *Chemical Lectures*, that genuine chemists ignored the study of primary corpuscles, their figures and mechanical principles, or forces, and concerned themselves with grosser principles evident to the senses and exhibited in the laboratory.[28] William Lewis, translator of the *Chemical Works* of Stahl's disciple, Caspar Neuman, in 1759, observed in his *Commercium Philosophico-Technicum* of 1763 that chemistry and the mechanical philosophy must be distinguished from one another, chemical phenomena not being reducible to mathematical calculation of mechanical principles.

By the time Priestley seriously began chemical experimentation there was a fairly well established view that chemistry was a very different subject from mechanical philosophy, and that its laws were not to be reduced to those of physics. William Cullen and Joseph Black, the two primary figures in British chemistry of that period, represent this view more impressively, perhaps, than the less important Shaw and Lewis. Cullen, who praised Stahl and the Stahlian Juncker in his chemical lectures, declares:

> The qualities that chemistry considers are different from those which mechanics or the mathematical philosophy considers. To regard attraction as proportional to particle density is purely speculative, for we know nothing of the figure of the small parts of bodies.[30]

Black is even more explicit. A student of Cullen, he too admired Stahl, but preferred the more sophisticated Stahlian approach of Pierre Joseph Macquer as a text for his students. Black pointedly rejects the "extravagant lengths" of Dr. Freind and his *Chemical Lectures,* and, while Black praises Newton in the customary British obeisance to the Grand Master, he also declares that chemical science is obstructed by speculations that attempt to explain chemical operations by attractions and repulsions.[31] Both Cullen and Black pursued chemistry as a series of material taxonomic problems. Why then does Priestley, in the midst of an antimechanist thrust to chemistry, pick up, after some forty-three years, the physicalist approach of Stephen Hales? What is the origin of his physicalist declaration in *The Doctrine of Philosophical Necessity Illustrated* of 1777? "Chemistry. . .and common mechanics are very different things; and accordingly we have different *kinds of laws* or *rules*, by which to express, and explain operations, but still they are equally branches of physics."[32]

Probably a single answer to such questions cannot be found, particularly since Priestley's physicalism was not a constant quality but increased from a generalized concern with the physical nature of matter in the 1760s, to explicit application of mechanistic explanations in the late 1770s. A number of partial and related answers suggest themselves, however, when Priestley's scientific work is viewed in a context that includes his early education in science and metaphysics and his later writings on nonscientific subjects. Priestley's first approach to science was through a program of self-education during which he read, and repeated the experiments described in, the *Mathematical Elements of Natural Philosophy Confirm'd by Experiment* of the Dutch Newtonian mechanist Willem Jacob 'sGravesande. First published in 1720-21, this was already an old-fashioned text by the time of the appearance of its sixth edition of 1747, shortly before Priestley read it. When he entered the dissenting academy at Daventry in 1752, Priestley was introduced to a more formal course of scientific studies, but this also appears to have been somewhat old-fashioned. The curricula and texts were much the same as those selected by the founder of the school, Philip Doddridge, in the late 1730s and early 1740s. Of the specific science texts Priestley used, one can identify only 'Boerhaave's Chemistry'' (probably in the English edition of 1753, but originally dating from a set of lectures given prior to 1724) and the *Compendious System of Natural Philosophy* by John Rowning, first published in parts between 1734 and 1743.[33] Of these two, Rowning seems to have been the more important to the future chemist. Boerhaave is seldom referred to, directly or indirectly, while Rowning's physicalist theory of matter was at least one source of the model which Priestley was frequently to adopt.

Rowning was a consistent reductionist, explaining all

phenomena in terms of particle mechanics, and even rejecting Newton's own aetherial explanation of diffraction rings with the declaration that the time would come when principles of attraction and repulsion would be found sufficient for that as well. He cites Hales with admiration and adopts the concept of homogeneous particles exhibiting both attraction and repulsion. Indeed, in one instance he suggests that a fundamental particle might be surrounded by as many as three concentric shells of alternate repulsive and attractive influence. Matter itself, however, is fundamentally inert, and the forces are actually evidence of the comtinued action of God in the universe.[34]

It is this interpretation of force as a manifestation of the omnipresent Deity that recommended Rowning to the attention of the theologically oriented academy masters and connects Priestley's formal scientific studies to that other new element of his education at Daventry, the study of metaphysics. This, too, seems to have been old-fashioned, in form as well as substance, being based on a set of as yet unpublished lectures by Doddridge on pneumatology, ethics, and divinity. The form of the lectures is curiously scholastic, with a series of questions on the relation of mind, body, soul, and God, which had exercised theologians during the first two decades of the eighteenth century. The answers to these questions are derived from the Cambridge Neoplatonists of the late seventeenth century and from the early Boyle lecturers, who had formulated the view of an omnipresent God continually acting, according to precise geometrical law, through forces in the universe. This combination of science and metaphysics early convinced Priestley that the most important problem in philosophy was the investigation of matter-force-spirit relationships.

There was, however, little explicit sign of this concern in Priestley's first published work in science, the *History and Present State of Electricity* of 1767. The dominant contemporary electrical theory was that of a single fluid, and Priestley faithfully describes its development. In doing so he combined the personal assistance of William Watson and Benjamin Franklin, and a bibliography of more than thirty items, into a successful and historically valuable study. Only in his rejection of an effluvial-atmosphere theory of electrical action and in his unexpected and generally unappreciated deduction of the electrical force law might one suspect that Priestley disagreed with his mentors in being a mechanist when they were materialists. And only by suspecting Priestley's physicalist bias would one see the tendencies of his own original electrical experiments on conductivities as application of mechanical considerations to a study of the motion of electrical fluid. Then, his dominant philosophical interest breaks through:

> Hitherto philosophy has been chiefly conversant about the more sensible properties of bodies: electricity, together with chymistry, and the doctrine of light and colours, seems to be giving us an inlet into their internal structure, on which all their sensible properties depend.[36]

During the next five years Priestley continued his electrical experiments, commenced seriously those on air, and began the work on a history of experimental philosophy that culminated in the *History and Present State of Discoveries Relating to Vision, Light, and Colours* (usually called the *History of Optics*) of 1772. This subject was not suited to Priestley's talents, and the book was not successful, but writing it did remind him of Rowning, from whose work he borrowed some plates and from whom he paraphrased the distrust of aetherial hypotheses for his preface. He also demonstrated that a dynamic mechanical explanation of Newton's Rings *could* be found in an elaboration of Rowning's hypothesis of concentric spheres of attraction and repulsion. This elaboration was the work of John Michell, a mechanist geologist and astronomer, and was based on a theory of the Abbé Roger Joseph Boscovich, who conceived (possibly independently of Rowning) the ultimate particles of matter as geometrical points surrounded by alternate spherical shells of repulsion and attraction. Boscovich's theory, which was to intrigue British scientists as late as the early twentieth century, supplied Priestley with the ultimate physicalist model of matter, which he was to use repeatedly in his metaphysical and theological writings, though there is little overt suggestion of it in his other scientific writings.[37]

In these, indeed, there is scarcely more mechanical reductionism immediately after the publication of the *History of Optics* than there had been in the scientific papers preceeding it. Some of the electrical papers suggest experiments opposing change-of-momentum concepts to transfer of substance, but as electrical researches give way to pneumatic studies, materialist theories predominate—as they had in the chemistry works of Neumann, Macquer, Macbride, Brownrigg, and Black that he had been reading from at least as early as 1766. This pattern of materialist-focused chemistry was inevitably reinforced in the chemistry works (fifty-five in all), which were among the two hundred and sixty-five titles Priestley had collected for his history of experimental philosophy.[38] Then, amid books by authors such as Stahl, Juncker, Waller, Shaw, and Lewis, there comes unexpectedly after thirty-one years the publication of a fourth edition of Stephen Hales's *Vegetable Staticks* in 1769.

The mechanism of Hales's chemistry might well have been swamped in the more contemporary version of material taxonomy. That this did not entirely happen testifies to the intensity and tenacity of Priestley's concern with theological fundamentals relating to the nature of matter. But it still comes as no surprise to discover that Priestley's first published pneumatic research paper, after "taking up. . .Dr. Hales's inquiries," the magisterial paper of 1772, is noteably ambivalent in its theoretical implications. The mode of the investigations—collecting the "airs" released from substances by heating or by mixture with acids or alkalies— is certainly consistent with the Hales "distillation" and "fermentation" techniques, and Priestley's metric of pressure and volume changes reflects the mechanical parameters of Hales chemical theory. The vocabulary also is often that of Hales—the "releasing" of airs from substances in which they have existed in an "unelastic state," for example—while Priestley is constantly employing physical means—rarefaction and compression, exposure to light or heat, agitation over water to see if the nature of the airs can be changed. But that experimental mode is not uncommon by Priestley's day, the vocabulary is equally marked with materialist phrases—"constitution" of the air and proportional quantities of substances, for example—and the physicalist experiments were conducted to *disprove* mechanist explanations. Air was not "restored" by condensation or rarefaction; no effect was noted after exposure of air to light or heat. Hales was wrong in supposing diminution was the result of decreased elasticity, for the lesser volume has less, not greater, specific gravity. Perhaps only in the suggestion that inflammability may be the result of "some particular mode or combination" of substances otherwise not inflammable is there any unequivocal suggestion of the physicalist explanations that play so obvious a role in the *History of Optics* published earlier the same year.[39]

The same ambivalence is, of course, to be found in the earliest volumes of Priestley's *Experiments and Observations on Different Kinds of Air*. The momentum of an indubitably successful mode of experimentation would, in itself, be sufficient explanation of this theoretical ambiguity, while there is nothing in contemporary scientific attitudes or discoveries to justify a change in Priestley's thinking. Nonetheless, it appears that each volume successively represents a stronger affinity for mechanistic explanation and for emphasis on the fundamental nature of matter. The first volume, of 1774, is half a reprinting of the 1772 paper and half an accounting of research done since that paper had been published. The general subject matter is the same, but there is some increased emphasis on differing modes of combination in addition to different proportional quantities of substances, as responsible for variations in properties. Here also there seems to be proposed the notion of phlogiston as a near primary form of matter, modifiable into electricity or light but not into heat, which, instead, is the subtle vibratory motion of the parts of bodies in action and reaction with one another.[40]

Volume 2, of 1775, announces the discovery of vitriolic acid air, fluoracid air, and first describes, in book form, the processes of discovery leading to the identification of dephlogisticated air. There can be no doubt that these discoveries, like those of nitrous air, dephlogisticated nitrous air, nitrous acid air, marine acid air, and alkaline air previously announced, are the results of a systematic program of experimentation based, but not uniquely dependent, upon the Halesian process of releasing fixed airs to their elastic state. The discoveries are, in a general sense then, not accidents. Indeed, the discovery of oxygen was almost inevitable from the time, late in 1772, when Priestley noted that the air released from nitre showed "'extraordinary and important properties.'"[41]

The psychology of discovery is a complicated one, and it would be hard to demonstrate any one-to-one relationship between the comparatively simple manipulative processes that produced the new gases and the theoretical insights that permitted Priestley to recognize what he had produced. That the theory, though still uncertain, is increasingly mechanistic is, however, clear from the preface to volume 2:

> . . .this is not now a business of air only, as it was at first, but appears to be of much greater magnitude and extent, so as to diffuse light upon the most general principles of natural knowledge, and especially those about which chymistry is particularly conversant. . . .we may perhaps discover principles of more extensive influence than even that of gravity itself. . .[42]

That Priestley means by these "principles of. . .extensive influence" those general mechanical Principles of Motion called for by Newton in the *Principia* and the *Optics* seems clear enough; their relation to his concern with the nature of matter is revealed in the preface to the third volume of *Experiments and Observations*, published in 1777. Here Priestley discloses that his expectations of "unfolding some of the most curious secrets of nature" is based on the belief that by "exhibiting substances *in the form of air*," they could be examined in a state less compounded and therefore one step nearer their primitive elements or particles. A general theory of different kinds of air would, in his opinion, describe not only the several ingredients that enter into their composition, but also the cause of their combination in the form of air and the reasons for their being resolved into other substances with other properties.[43]

Priestley was not, however, to describe such a "general theory of different kinds of air" in this third volume, nor indeed in any of the subsequent volumes he produced. The 1777 volume nonetheless represents the completion of a major stage in his researches. He declares his intention, in its preface, of discontinuing his researches in "this branch of experimental philosophy," for his "attention will be sufficiently engaged by speculations of a very different nature." When the fourth volume appeared in 1779, it commenced a new series with the title changed to *Experiments and Observations Relating to Various Branches of Natural Philosophy*.[44] The new series does continue *"Observations on Air"* and many of these differ little from those of earlier volumes. However, there is a marked new interest in what, for the nineteenth or twentieth centuries, would be called transport phenomena: variations in gaseous diffusion rates with specific gravity, temperature, and pressure, and conductivities of heat and sound. These were not, however, the "speculations of a different nature" about which he had spoken earlier, for these are identified as "of a metaphysical nature" in the preface to that fourth volume. Yet it was these metaphysical speculations that were responsible for the change, and that, indeed, must be given the primary responsibility for the steady progress of Priestley's convictions toward the final stage of a theory of matter which he attained by 1777. No doubt the successes of his pneumatic investigations contributed toward this final definition of a dynamic mechanical theory of matter, but one cannot ignore that those years between 1774 and 1777, which saw the publication of the first three volumes of *Experiments and Observations,* also saw the publication of three out of four of Priestley's major metaphysical works: the *Examination* of Scottish Common Sense Philosophy of 1774; the introductory essays to his edition of David Hartley's *Theory of the Human Mind* of 1775; and, most significantly, the *Disquisitions relating to Matter and Spirit* of 1777. All three of these works are designedly of theological concern, and it is not the function of this essay to discuss the relationship of Priestley's theology to his science. It must be emphasized, however, that it was in those three works that Priestley explicitly defined the theory of matter and its action that provided the ontological basis for his pneumatic epistemology.

That theory of matter took its most determinate (and extreme) form however, in the 1778 *Free Discussion of the Doctrines of Materialism and Philosophical Necessity.* Suppose, Priestley suggests, that the Divine Being, in creating matter, "only fixed certain *centers of various attractions and repulsions,* extending indefinitely in all direction, these centers approaching to, or receding from each other, and consequently carrying their peculiar spheres of attraction and repulsion along with them . . ." A complex of these centers, placed within one another's spheres of attraction, would constitute a solid body, which could be divided to near infinity without destruction of the characteristic matter, as each division, regardless of how small, would still leave a part containing many centers: " . . . matter is, by this means, resolved into nothing but the *divine* agency, exerted according to certain rules."[45]

There is nothing startlingly new in this theory of matter; it is merely a refined version of the dynamic corpuscular hypothesis of particles in motion, with forces of attraction and repulsion between them, which Priestley had learned indirectly from Newton and directly from Rowning and Hales. That his version of it had profound metaphysical and theological consequences seems clear, but the explicit application of it to pneumatic studies did not prompt major changes in experimental procedures or interpretations. Priestley may, however, have felt somewhat more free to divulge the ultimate nature of the physicalist speculations inherent in his scientific work with this disclosure of his metaphysical ideas. In the 1779 volume of *Experiments and Observations* he describes an attempt to convert water into earth by heating it under pressure, hoping to extend the spheres of attraction of the water particles to intersection by preventing the particles from receding from one another under influence of their spheres of repulsion.[46] During the years 1782-83 he became convinced that he had attained the opposite effect, the transformation of water into permanent air, by rarifying its particles beyond their spheres of attraction into a stable sphere of repulsion.[47] Each of these efforts has overtones of the Abbé Boscovich's matter theory about which Priestley had written in 1772, though they may harken back instead to the Rowning he had read in 1752. In any event, the theory is consistent with that outlined in the *Disquisitions relating to Matter and Spirit,* and it explains both the role that Priestley was to play in the discovery of the compound nature of water *and* his persistent refusal to accept the conclusions of that discovery.

Indeed the theory and its implications explain much about Priestley's reluctance to accept the new chemical theory of Lavoisier. In 1794 Priestley published his *Heads of Lectures on a Course of Experimental Philosophy.* In those lectures he describes the circumstances that cause changes in the properties of bodies as: (1) the addition of substances, or things that are the objects of our senses, (2) changes of structure of the substance itself, and (3) the addition of something not the object of our senses—such as magnetization.[48] As he later defines the nature of all substance as extension and powers of attraction and repulsion, it seems clear that he could not have accepted mere addition of substance as an ultimate explanation of change. The incompleteness of such explanations is what he had in mind when he wrote to Martin van Marum, in August 1790, about differences in experimental results of water composition experiments:

I do not . . . question the result of Mr. Berthollet's experiment. He is too cautious a man to be deceived, but I imagine more than we were aware of depends on the different methods of combining the two kinds of air.[49]

Priestley wanted more than a set of compositional recipes. He wrote:

I cannot conclude . . . without observing that the advances we are continually making in the analyses of natural substances into the elements of which they consist, bring us but one step nearer to their constitutional differences, since as much depends upon the mode of arrangment, concerning which we know nothing at all, as upon the elements themselves . . . .[50]

Now this is *not* physical chemistry. The major experimental results disputed by Priestley were resolved by Lavoisian analytical chemistry and did not depend upon differences in mode, arrangement, structure, or any of the other physical parameters that Priestley required. But this *is* physicalist chemistry, with that reductionist impulse to reduce chemical phenomena to problems of mechanics which, a century later—after the intervention of kinetic theory, organic chemistry, and electro-chemistry—would make the more general questions raised by Priestley less premature. And it was the same kind of physicalist chemistry that traced its origins back to Robert Boyle, which minimized combinations of substances as explanation for phenomena. Compare the two quotations:

Indeed, a knowledge of the elements which enter into the composition of natural substances, is but a small part of what it is desireable to investigation with respect to them, the principle, and the mode of their combination, as how it is that they become hard or soft, elastic or nonelastic, solid or fluid, is quite another subject.[51]

How indestructible soever the chymical principles be supposed, divers of the operations ascribed to them will never be well made out, without the help of motion, (and that diversified too;) without which, we can little better give an account of the phaenomena of many bodies, by knowing wht ingredients compose them, than we can explain the operations of a watch, by knowing how many and what metals, the balance, the wheels, the chain, and other parts are made.[52]

Two expressions of the same thought—the first by Joseph Priestley, in a last defiant argument against the new chemistry of material substances, in 1802; the second by Robert Boyle, in the *Excellency and Grounds of the Corpuscular or Mechanical Philosophy*, in 1674.

Priestley's ultimate failure, I submit, had the same roots as his earlier successes. Neither relate simply to an understanding of the concepts or the techniques of analytical chemistry—or to their lack. Both derive from a too sophisticated endeavor to answer questions that his contemporaries were not asking, with concepts so antique they would not again be modern for nearly one hundred years.

NOTES

1. Joseph Priestley to Theophilus Lindsey, 21 February 1770, in John Towill Rutt, ed., *Life and Correspondence of Joseph Priestley* (London: R. Hunter, 1831-32), vol. 1, pt. 1, pp. 112-14.
2. I have used: Stephen Hales, *Statical Essays: Containing Vegetable Staticks...*, 3d. ed. with amendments, (London: W. Innys, R. Manby, T. Woodward, J. Peele, 1738). There has been a reprint of the first edition (London: Oldbourne Book Co., Ltd., 1961), but the third edition is closer in text to the fourth, and last edition of 1769, which is the form in which Priestley saw it. See his "Catalogue of Books" appended to the *History and Present State of Discoveries Relating to Vision, Light, and Colours* (London: J. Johnson, 1772).
3. For its influence on eighteenth century chemists, see Henry Guerlac, "The Continental Reputation of Stephen Hales," *Archives Internationales d'Histoire des Sciences* 4 (1951): 393-404. Note that treatment of air as a fluid was common in the late seventeenth and early eighteenth centuries, for which see Alexandre Koyré, "Pascal Savant," in *Metaphysics and Measurement* (London: Chapman Hall, 1968), pp. 152-56.
4. See any of the writings of Marie Boas Hall on Boyle, and particularly Marie Boas [Hall], "The Establishment of the Mechanical Philosophy," *Osiris* 10 (1952): 413-541.
5. Selection quoted in Marie Boas Hall, *Robert Boyle on Natural Philosophy, An Essay with Selections from His Writings* (Bloomington, Ind.: Indiana University Press, 1965), p. 199.

6. "Introduction" to the *Mechanical Origin and Production of Qualities,* in Hall, *Boyle on Natural Philosophy,* p. 242.
7. From Hall, *Boyle on Natural Philosophy,* p. 247.
8. Described in J. R. Partington, *A History of Chemistry* (London: Macmillan & Co., Ltd, 1962), 3: 33.
9. G. Homberg, "Essais de Chimie," *Memoires de l'Academie des Sciencès* (for 1702, Amsterdam ed., 1737), pp. 57-58, and "Sur une dissolution d'Argent," *Histoire de l'Academie Royale des Sciences* (for 1706, Paris ed., 1777), pp. 49-50.
10. Isaac Newton, *Sir Isaac Newton's Mathematical Principles of Natural Philosophy and his System of the World,* trans. Andrew Motle, ed. Florian Cajori (Berkeley, Calif.: University of California Press, 1947), p. xviii.
11. Query 23 of the 1706 Latin *Optice* becomes Query 31 in the second English edition of 1718, *Opticks: or, A Treatise of the Reflections, Refractions, Inflections, and Colours of Light* (London: W. and J. Innys, 1718), pp. 375-76.
12. Newton, *Opticks,* p. 377.
13. John Keill, "In qua Leges Attractionis alique Physices Principia traduntur," *Philosophical Transactions* 26 (1708-9): 97-110; translated in Hutton, Shaw, Pearson, et al., eds., *Philosophical Transactions Abridged* (London, 1809), 5: 407-24.
14. John Freind, *Praelectiones Chemicae* translated as *Chymical Lectures* (London, for Jonah Bowyer, 1712).
15. Freind, *Chymical Lectures,* pp. 96-101.
16. Hales, *Vegetable Staticks,* p. vii.
17. Roger Cotes's lectures were posthumously published, *Hydrostatical and Pneumatical Lectures* (London, 1738).
18. See [Francis Hauksbee and William Whiston], *A Course of Mechanical, Optical, Hydrostatical, and Pneumatical Experiments* (London, n.p., 1714), which Whiston tells us was based on the experiments done for Cotes's course in 1707, *Memoirs of the Life of Mr. William Whiston* (London, 1749), 1: 136-37, 235-36.
19. Cotes, *Lectures,* Lecture 16, pp. 202-3.
20. Hales, *Vegetable Staticks,* p. 314.
21. For Mickleburgh's lectures, see Robert E. Schofield, *Mechanism and Materialism* (Princeton, N.J.: Princeton University Press, 1970), pp. 47-49.
22. See Tenney L. Davis, "Vicissitudes of Boerhaave's Textbook of Chemistry," *Isis* 10 (1928): 33-46.
23. Hales, *Vegetable Staticks,* pp. 193-98; Henry Guerlac, "Joseph Black and Fixed Air: A Bicentenary Retrospective. . . .," *Isis* 48 (1957): 124-51; 433-56.
24. Hales, *Vegetable Staticks,* p. 287.
25. Stephen Hales, *Statical Essays: Containing Haemastaticks* &c, facs. rpt. of 1733 ed., no. 22, History of Medicine Series, N.Y. Academy of Medicine (New York: Hafner Publishing Co., 1964), pp. 318-19.

26. Pieter van Musschenbroek, *Elements of Natural Philosophy*, trans. John Colson (London: J. Nourse, 1744), 1: 198-204. English translation of 1734, Latin ed.
27. Herman Boerhaave, *A New Method of Chemistry*, trans. Peter Shaw (London, 1753), third edition (essentially same as 2d edn of 1741), note, pp. 156-57.
28. Peter Shaw, *Chemical Lectures* (London, 1755), pp. 146-47.
29. William Lewis, *Commercium Philosophico-Technicum*, quoted by L. Trengrove, "Chemistry at the Royal Society of London in the Eighteenth Century—I," *Annals of Science* 19 (1963): 191-92.
30. See William P. D. Wightman, "William Cullen and the Teaching of Chemistry—II," *Annals of Science* 12 (1956): 194.
31. Joseph Black, *Lectures on the Elements of Chemistry* (Edinburgh, 1803), 1: 282-83.
32. Joseph Priestley, *The Doctrine of Philosophical Necessity Illustrated* (London, 1777), p. 283.
33. For Priestley's reading at Daventry, see Robert E. Schofield, ed., *A Scientific Autobiography of Joseph Priestley* (Cambridge, Mass.: MIT Press, 1966), p. 6.
34. See Schofield, *Mechanism and Materialism*, pp. 34-39 for an account of John Rowning and his work.
35. Posthumously published as Philip Doddridge, *A Course of Lectures on the Principle Subjects in Pneumatology, Ethics and Divinity* (London, 1763).
36. Joseph Priestley, *The History and Present State of Electricity*, rpt. of 3d ed. of 1775 in vol. 1: (N. Y. Johnson Reprint, 1966): xiv-xv; vol. 2: 70-80.
37. Joseph Priestley, *History and Present State of Discoveries relating to Vision, Light, and Colours* [History of Optics] (London, 1772), pp. viii, 392.
38. See "Catalogue of Books, of which Dr. Priestley is already possessed or to which he has access," appended to the *History of Optics*.
39. Joseph Priestley, "Observations on Different Kinds of Air," read March 5, 12, 19, 26, 1772, *Philosophical Transactions* 62 (1772): 233.
40. Joseph Priestley, *Experiments and Observations on Different Kinds of Air*, 2d ed. (London, 1775), 1: 280, 281.
41. Joseph Priestley, "Observations," p. 246.
42. Joseph Priestley, *Experiments and Observations*, 2d ed. (London, 1776), 2: vii-viii.
43. Joseph Priestley, *Experiments and Observations* (London, 1777), 3: ix-x.
44. Ibid., p. vii.
45. Joseph Priestley and Richard Price, *A Free Discussion of the Doctrines of Materialism and Philosophical Necessity* (London, 1778), pp. 247-50.
46. Joseph Priestley, *Experiments and Observations* (London, 1779), 4: 408.

47. Letter 100, Joseph Priestley to Josiah Wedgwood, 8 December 1782, *Scientific Autobiography.*
48. Joseph Priestley, *Heads of Lectures on a Course of Experimental Philosophy* (London, 1794), pp. 4-5.
49. Letter 136, Joseph Priestley to Martin van Marum, 21 August 1790, *Scientific Autobiography.*
50. Joseph Priestley, *Experiments on the Generation of Air from Water* (London, 1793), pp. 38-39.
51. Joseph Priestley, "Miscellaneous Observations Relating to the Doctrine of Air," *New York Medical Repository* 5 (1802): 264-67.
52. Robert Boyle, "Of the Excellency and Grounds of the Corpuscular or Mechanical Philosophy," in Hall, *Boyle on Natural Philosophy*, p. 201.